52 WEEKS
in the WORD

52 WEEKS
in the WORD

⋄

A COMPANION FOR READING
THROUGH THE BIBLE IN A YEAR

⋄

TRILLIA J. NEWBELL

MOODY PUBLISHERS
CHICAGO

Edited by Amanda Cleary Eastep
Interior illustrations by Kaylee Dunn
Interior and cover design: Erik M. Peterson
Cover illustration of landscape copyright © 2021 by Xenia Artwork/iStock (1297492616).
Interior illustrations copyright © 2021 Xenia Artwork/iStock (mountains: 1299465379, mountains: 1299850614, plants: 1309236761).
Interior illustrations copyright © 2022 Xenia Artwork/Shutterstock (mountains: 1906795684).
Interior illustrations copyright © 2022 Nadia Grapes/Shutterstock (tribal pattern: 1389285218, leaves/shapes: 1756747541, abstract florals: 1858737874, abstract leaves: 1859693353, leaves: 1907453473, mountain/leaves: 1947830434, abstract lines: 2142737565).
Interior illustrations copyright © 2022 Reuki/Shutterstock (minimalist cutouts: 1758818747, torn shapes: 1771306325).
All rights reserved for all illustrations above.
Author photo: Photography by Parker Plott

Library of Congress Cataloging-in-Publication Data

Names: Newbell, Trillia J., author.
Title: 52 weeks in the word : a companion for reading through the Bible in
  a year / Trillia Newbell.
Other titles: Fifty-two weeks in the word
Description: Chicago : Moody Publishers, [2022] | Includes bibliographical
  references. | Summary: "Join Trillia on a joy-filled, thoughtful, and
  realistic pathway through the entirety of God's Word! She'll help you
  organize and pause for deeper meditation. You'll discover treasures-some
  old, some new-help for daily living, hope in times of suffering, and an
  abiding relationship with the God who loves you"-- Provided by
  publisher.
Identifiers: LCCN 2022018598 (print) | LCCN 2022018599 (ebook) | ISBN
  9780802428356 | ISBN 9780802475589 (ebook)
Subjects: LCSH: Bible--Reading. | Bible--Devotional literature. | BISAC:
  RELIGION / Christian Living / Spiritual Growth | RELIGION / Christian
  Living / Devotional
Classification: LCC BS617 .N49 2022 (print) | LCC BS617 (ebook) | DDC
  220.6/1--dc23/eng/20220615
LC record available at https://lccn.loc.gov/2022018598
LC ebook record available at https://lccn.loc.gov/2022018599

Originally delivered by fleets of horse–drawn wagons, the affordable paperbacks from D. L. Moody's publishing house resourced the church and served everyday people. Now, after more than 125 years of publishing and ministry, Moody Publishers' mission remains the same—even if our delivery systems have changed a bit. For more information on other books (and resources) created from a biblical perspective, go to www.moodypublishers .com or write to:

Moody Publishers
820 N. LaSalle Boulevard
Chicago, IL 60610

1 3 5 7 9 10 8 6 4 2

Printed in the United States of America

To the Lord who redeemed my life from the pit
and crowned me with steadfast love and mercy

Contents

Introduction:
Reading the Bible for Our Joy

L iteracy means competence or knowledge in a specific area. Therefore, Bible literacy is competence or knowledge in the Bible. Simple enough. However, studies show that most Americans who own Bibles don't actually read them.[1] If you've picked up this book, there's a couple things I can assume: 1) You love God and love His Word, or 2) you want to grow in your love of God and love for His Word. Your desire is to become Bible literate.

That's likely an oversimplification of who you are. You might also be someone who feels guilty because you've tried to read the Bible but can't seem to make it a daily part of your life, so you need some help. Or maybe you have never read the Bible at all and wanted to take on a yearlong challenge—make a New Year's resolution. Perhaps you've received this book as a gift and you're not sure if you'll keep reading (I hope you do, and I pray it *will* be a gift to you!). Whatever has led you here, you've come to hold it in your hand, and I'm grateful because it will lead you to the most important book you own.

I believe you and I fall into both of my simplified categories. You and I likely love God and love His Word *and* we desire to grow in love of God and His Word.

Anytime we set out to do something big—like read the Bible in a year!— it's easy to start a journey with doubts. We've failed before we even begin.

That's why before I get into the nitty-gritty of how to use this read-through-the-Bible resource, I want to ease any of your doubts. None of us have arrived. We all find ourselves struggling from time to time to read the Bible and interpret it correctly. There will be many of you who begin reading and then have to coach yourself to keep going. You'll start and stop and start again. And here's the good news: that's okay. Not only is it okay, it's great. The goal of this book isn't to win some race or prize; we don't earn more favor before the Lord. The goal of this book is to provide one more resource to help you get in the Word, stay in the Word, and gain biblical literacy.

WHAT THIS IS NOT

Most authors don't want you to know what their book is *not* before you even begin! But I want you to know so that you 1) have the right expectations, and 2) understand that you get to do the work. I've had the joy of writing several Bible studies. Bible studies take the reader on a deep dive into the text. Studies like that help the reader observe, interpret, and apply the text. I'll continue to write Bible studies, Lord willing, but as I taught them, I realized that there's a knowledge base that was assumed. It was a baseline knowledge and understanding of the storyline of Scripture. Some have said that the New Testament interprets the Old, and as I taught these lessons, I would hear myself saying, "If you've read Genesis, you know . . ." or "As you know, the Hebrew midwives . . ."

Here's the thing, I can't keep it all straight, and that's not what I'm suggesting you do. I get confused by all the men whose names begin with "J" (seriously, Jacob, Joshua, Joseph, etc. So many Js!). I can remember overall themes but may forget minute details. (How many friends did Job have, three or four? Does it matter? Not sure.) But the only way to understand what is going on and how it all connects is to read the whole Bible. It's all connected. Reading the Gospels and the book of Hebrews, for example, only truly make sense if you've read the Old Testament. You won't and don't need to know every fact and historical event, but we could benefit from learning to read the whole rather than returning to our favorite book and only reading that book over and over again. I confess, I've read the book of Romans and Ephesians maybe a hundred times, but Malachi maybe three times.

So, what is this not? It's not a yearlong Bible study. The goal is Bible reading. It is a journal, a cheerleader, and a guide to help *you* continue reading. I am your Bible reading accountability partner. This isn't a summary of the Bible (although those are wonderful resources)—I want *you* to read the Bible. This isn't a line-by-line study with inductive questions (you'll have time for that if you'd like to pause. More on that below). Ultimately, my hope is that as you read God's Word, you will grow more in love with the Savior and eager to learn more about Him.

As we seek to delight in God, it's important to clarify that our reading time is *not* about earning His approval or favor. Trying to do so leads to the pitfall of legalism in our worship: pursuing good works with the intention of earning God's favor. An example of legalism is reading Scripture so that God will love you and be pleased with you and to ensure your standing with Him would be secure. When we work hard in order to earn God's favor, we are not operating with faith. Instead, we are saying that we must add to the finished work of Jesus on the cross; that His work wasn't enough, and therefore we must work to make Him happy by, in this case, spending time delighting in His Word.

The good news is that *52 Weeks in the Word* is also not about earning God's approval. We already have it!

GETTING OUR HEARTS READY

One of God's sweetest gifts, besides Himself, is His Word. Scripture is God-breathed. Both the Old and New Testaments are His words that reveal Him to us (2 Peter 1:21). The Scriptures are useful, binding, relevant, and true (2 Tim. 3:16–17). The law is perfect and revives the soul (Ps. 19:7). The Lord uses His Word to bring people to Himself (Rom. 10:17). God has been gracious to give you and me access to know many things about Him: His creation, His desires for us, and, most important, His Son. Are we reading and treasuring this precious gift? This book is a tool to help you do just that.

I have had seasons of Spirit-filled, worshipful, and consistent times in the Word and seasons when reading has felt like a duty rather than a joy and delight. I've had seasons when I've gotten up at five in the morning to read, study, and pray. And I have had seasons when I was happy just to get in the shower and feed the kids. So, we can all acknowledge that there are times in life when reading the Bible is tough even though we long to.

I have some good news and maybe some bad news: we aren't necessarily after spiritual highs every time we engage God's Word. If you approach the Word with the mindset that if you don't *feel* something, then you aren't *getting* anything from it, you won't read it. Once you change the focus from yourself to God, it's not only proper but it's also freeing. You will need to remind yourself of this truth when we get into the depths of Leviticus or begin reading all of the names in 1 Chronicles. We find joy in Scripture, not because it makes us feel good but because it leads us to the One who spoke it into existence.[2]

Now that we understand the heart behind it and the posture with which we hope to approach this reading plan, let's learn how to use it.

LET'S GET STARTED

Over the next 52 weeks (doesn't 52 weeks sound easier than 365 days?), you'll have:

1. Daily Scripture readings
2. Daily reflection questions (the same ones to make it easier to keep going!)
3. Prayer prompts and space for writing your own prayer
4. A weekly reflection on a portion of text from the assigned reading (These will vary because the goal is Bible reading, and this is a supplement, not a substitute.)
5. A day of rest on the last day of the week

The 52 weeks are designed to be read sequentially; however, if you miss a week, simply start where you last stopped. In other words, it's a 52-week read-through of the Bible that you can adapt for your needs.

The Daily Readings

This reading plan is meant to take you from Genesis to Revelation in a few chapters each day for 365 days. There are no rules for how you read it or what time of day you read it. Some of you may choose to listen to your Bible on your daily walk. Others may wake up at five o'clock in the morning and read before the sun comes up. Still others of you may read daily before you go to bed. It's up to you. No rules.

If you would like a look at what you'll be reading each day, you will find the reading plan chart in the back of the book.

Daily Reflection Questions

Each day I ask you to consider the same three questions:

1. What do you learn about God and His character in these verses?
2. Where is Jesus in these chapters? Where do you see the gospel?
3. How might you apply these verses to your life?

The Bible is about God, so I wanted to help you think about what you just read and what it says about God. And you may have heard the phrase "Jesus is on every page," or that all Scripture points to our Savior. The more I read, the more I find this to be true. Plus, Jesus made the same claim (John 5:39)! I have a desire for us to remember the Lord and His gospel every day. The second question helps us think about how Jesus might be reflected, foreshadowed, or explicitly addressed in the text. But don't force Him in there; it's okay when the questions don't apply clearly to the text. And finally, the Bible is to be read and lived. We'll want to think about how each of our readings apply to our life. Please note that this is not a test. These questions are meant to help you and me reflect, but if you get to a relatively obscure passage and you can't even begin to know how to reflect on it, maybe jot it down to return to at another time.

Prayer Prompts

52 Weeks in the Word is not a book about prayer. But if we desire a relationship with the Lord, we should speak to Him through prayer. And if we desire wisdom, we should ask (James 1:5). We should ask the Lord to illuminate His Word to us. We will surely need God's help to read, understand, and apply His Word! Let's ask Him for it.

A Weekly Reflection

At the end of each week, before you enter the Rest Day, you'll find reflections to help you refocus, pause, and think about an aspect of your reading that week, whether it's a devotional thought on a text, musings about the context, or a revelation illuminated through my own reading.

You'll be reading a lot. As your Bible reading companion and accountability partner, I want to pop in to encourage you but not overwhelm you with more reading. However, each short piece does assume that you've read the chapters for that week.

A Day of Rest

I admit that "a day of rest" sounds like I believe that Bible reading is work and we need to rest from it. The Rest Day at the end of each week isn't a rest from Bible reading; rather, it's a rest from this particular Bible reading plan. You can use that day to catch up on reading or dive deeper into a theological concept or text that caught your eye. It can be a time to read ahead if you'd like, or it might be a wonderful time to go back to the devotional to read and reflect. The day will not have a daily reading assignment, and so you are free to use it as you wish.

BUT DO I REALLY HAVE TIME?

Yes! You have more time than you think. And if you decide to use alternative methods such as listening to the Bible, you may be surprised by how much you are able to "read" in a year. There are many charts and estimates for how long it takes to complete each book of the Bible. But you can see from the list below, the majority of the books take less than one hour to read![3]

Estimated Reading Time (shortest to longest)[4]

BOOK	MINUTES
3 John	2.2
2 John	2.5
Philemon	3.5
Obadiah	4.5
Jude	4.6
Titus	7
2 Thessalonians	8
Nahum	8.5
Haggai	9
Habakkuk	10
Jonah	10
2 Peter	10
Zephaniah	10
2 Timothy	12
Malachi	13
Joel	15
1 Thessalonians	15
Colossians	16
1 Timothy	16
Philippians	16
1 Peter	17
James	17.5
Song of Songs	20
Ruth	20
Micah	21
1 John	21
Galatians	22
Lamentations	23
Ephesians	24
Amos	30
Hosea	36
2 Corinthians	45
Ecclesiastes	45

BOOK	MINUTES
Zechariah	48
Esther	49
Hebrews	50
Ezra	56
1 Corinthians	68
Romans	71
Nehemiah	85
Daniel	90
Revelation	98
Proverbs	99
Mark	113
Job	126
Judges	153
John	156
Joshua	156
1 Chronicles	166
2 Samuel	171
Matthew	183
Acts	184
2 Kings	187
Leviticus	188
Luke	194
1 Kings	203
1 Samuel	208
2 Chronicles	213
Deuteronomy	230
Numbers	250
Isaiah	256
Exodus	259
Ezekiel	299
Psalms	301
Genesis	320
Jeremiah	330

Now let's read the Bible!

·

·

Genesis 1
to
Genesis 28

Consider

1 What do you learn about God and His character in these verses?
2 Where is Jesus in these chapters? Where do you see the gospel?
3 How might you apply these verses to your life?

DAY 1 • *Read* Genesis 1–4

DAY 2 • *Read* Genesis 5–10

Say or write your prayer:

1 What do you learn about God and His character in these verses?
2 Where is Jesus in these chapters? Where do you see the gospel?
3 How might you apply these verses to your life?

DAY 3 • *Read* Genesis 11–16

DAY 4 • *Read* Genesis 17–20

Say or write your prayer:

1 What do you learn about God and His character in these verses?
2 Where is Jesus in these chapters? Where do you see the gospel?
3 How might you apply these verses to your life?

DAY 5 • *Read* Genesis 21–24

DAY 6 • *Read* Genesis 25–28

Say or write your prayer:

A Fast-Moving Start

Genesis moves quickly. In the first few chapters, we see God created the world, animals, and humans. In creating humans, the Lord did something that affected the way we interact with Him, view one another, and participate in the world: God created humans in His image (*imago Dei*). But then the first humans made a mess of things. After the fall of the first man and woman came shame, jealousy, sibling rivalry, murder, and death. Corruption rose on the earth, and God exacted His righteous justice. Just when it seemed all was lost, new life and promises—great and glorious promises— burst onto the scene. We could spend the rest of our days learning about the first few chapters of Genesis—the beginning of the epic story of redemption. God begins His display of love and mercy from the beginning: creating all things and calling them good, providing for and caring for our fallen ancestors. It's a great story—a true story—and we've only just begun.

I'm more convinced than ever that if you can grasp what's happening in Genesis, you'll better understand the entire Bible.

Let's keep reading!

**IDEAS
FOR YOUR
REST DAY**

Catch up on any missed reading.

Pause to study a text or chapter using your favorite Bible study method.

Identify a person or situation in the text, and learn more about their story.

Genesis 29
to
Genesis 50

Consider

1 What do you learn about God and His character in these verses?
2 Where is Jesus in these chapters? Where do you see the gospel?
3 How might you apply these verses to your life?

DAY 1 • *Read* Genesis 29–31

DAY 2 • *Read* Genesis 32–36

Say or write your prayer:

Consider

1 What do you learn about God and His character in these verses?
2 Where is Jesus in these chapters? Where do you see the gospel?
3 How might you apply these verses to your life?

DAY 3 • *Read* Genesis 37–40

DAY 4 • *Read* Genesis 41–43

Say or write your prayer:

1 What do you learn about God and His character in these verses?
2 Where is Jesus in these chapters? Where do you see the gospel?
3 How might you apply these verses to your life?

DAY 5 • *Read* Genesis 44–47

DAY 6 • *Read* Genesis 48–50

Say or write your prayer:

| *Unmerited Forgiveness*

The story of Joseph and his brothers is pretty wild. I can't imagine being sold into slavery by my own flesh and blood. What's odd is that the brothers seemed to think they were doing Joseph a favor by not killing him and instead selling him (Gen. 37:25–27). How often, I wonder, do we excuse our wrongdoings too? Who needs a television drama when you've got the book of Genesis? There are a lot of details in this story to help us understand the history of Israel; however, I was struck by Joseph's forgiveness of his brothers.

We often hear his words paraphrased: "What man planned for evil, God planned for good" (Gen. 50:19–20). What's remarkable is that Joseph had faith throughout *all* of his sufferings, even before he knew the end of the story. He didn't deny the Lord. His faith, from what we can tell, did not falter. And although Joseph's words have, unfortunately, become a cliché, we know they're true. We can rightly point to Romans 8:28 and proclaim, yes, all of God's plans are good and for our good!

But Joseph not only points us to the One he trusted to provide (God), Joseph also provided for his brothers (Gen. 50:21). He comforted them and spoke kindly to his brothers. Joseph's radical display of love and forgiveness points us to Jesus. Jesus not only forgives sin and pours out grace to the undeserving (Eph. 2: 8–10), He rewards those who follow Him (Heb. 11:6). Unmerited forgiveness, undeserved favor, unearned gifts—all are ours because of our Lord.

**IDEAS
FOR YOUR
REST DAY**

Catch up on any missed reading.

Pause to study a text or chapter using your favorite Bible study method.

Identify a person or situation in the text, and learn more about their story.

·

·

Exodus 1
to
Exodus 21

1 What do you learn about God and His character in these verses?
2 Where is Jesus in these chapters? Where do you see the gospel?
3 How might you apply these verses to your life?

DAY 1 • *Read* Exodus 1–4

DAY 2 • *Read* Exodus 5–8

Say or write your prayer:

1 What do you learn about God and His character in these verses?

2 Where is Jesus in these chapters? Where do you see the gospel?

3 How might you apply these verses to your life?

DAY 3 • *Read* Exodus 9–11

DAY 4 • *Read* Exodus 12–14

Say or write your prayer:

1 What do you learn about God and His character in these verses?
2 Where is Jesus in these chapters? Where do you see the gospel?
3 How might you apply these verses to your life?

DAY 5 • *Read* Exodus 15–17

DAY 6 • *Read* Exodus 18–21

Say or write your prayer:

God Judges

God is a God of justice. The Egyptians enslaved Israel. Pharaoh's heart was hardened, and he would not let the Israelites go. So, God displayed His justice through the plagues. Often, it seems, the plagues are told like a fairy tale—cartoonish Bible stories. But if we take a moment to consider all that we profess about the Word of God, then we must believe that these events not only happened but affected all of Egypt. I imagine if a water system turned to blood today, there'd be an outcry and sense of desperation; many would turn to God and pray for mercy. But no doubt there would be the questions: "Did God really do that?" "How could God be sovereign and allow this destruction?"

I don't pretend to know all of God's ways. As the hymn writer William Cowper wrote:

> *"God moves in a mysterious way,*
> *His wonders to perform;*
> *He plants His footsteps in the sea,*
> *And rides upon the storm."*[1]

His ways are not our ways (Isa. 55:8–9). And we know that God cannot sin, for He is righteous and holy. What is clear through the sending of the plagues and what appears to be the point is this: God is real and there is no one like our God (Ex. 7:17; 8:10; 9:14b).[2]

Understanding all of God's attributes enables us to worship Him rightly. Understanding the seriousness of sin against our holy, just God brings us to our knees in thanksgiving for Christ, our Passover Lamb (1 Cor. 5:7).

IDEAS FOR YOUR REST DAY

Catch up on any missed reading.

Pause to study a text or chapter using your favorite Bible study method.

Identify a person or situation in the text, and learn more about their story.

Three times in the year
a feast to me. You shall
of Unleavened Bread. A
you, you shall eat unleav
seven days at the appoi
month of Abib, for in it
of Egypt. None shall app
empty-handed. You sha
of Harvest, of the firstfr
labor, of what you sow i
shall keep the Feast of I
end of the year, when yo
the field the fruit of you
times in the year shall al
appear before the Lord

WEEK 4

Exodus 22
to
Exodus 40

1 What do you learn about God and His character in these verses?
2 Where is Jesus in these chapters? Where do you see the gospel?
3 How might you apply these verses to your life?

DAY 1 • *Read* Exodus 22–24

DAY 2 • *Read* Exodus 25–27

Say or write your prayer:

Consider

1 What do you learn about God and His character in these verses?
2 Where is Jesus in these chapters? Where do you see the gospel?
3 How might you apply these verses to your life?

DAY 3 • *Read* Exodus 28–30

DAY 4 • *Read* Exodus 31–34

Say or write your prayer:

1 What do you learn about God and His character in these verses?
2 Where is Jesus in these chapters? Where do you see the gospel?
3 How might you apply these verses to your life?

DAY 5 • _Read_ Exodus 35–37

DAY 6 • _Read_ Exodus 38–40

Say or write your prayer:

Sin Can't Be in His Presence

Exodus has a complicated ending. On the one hand, the tabernacle is completed and the people of God enjoy the power of God on display. In a brief but momentous mention, we read that Moses could not enter the tabernacle. Did you catch that in Exodus 40:35? Moses could not be in the presence of God's glory and power. What happened?

The people broke the first and second commandments of the Ten Commandments (see Ex. 32). God was angry and wanted to wipe out His people, and Moses, playing the role of mediator between the Israelites and God, appealed to the Lord. Moses asked the Lord to remember His covenant with Abraham and to consider how the Egyptians would view His actions (Ex. 32:11–13). The Lord heard Moses's pleas and relented. But the damage was done. When all was said and done, not even Moses could enter the tabernacle in Exodus 40 when God's glory filled it. Even though God was finally making a way for His people to access His presence, the laws, priesthood, sacrifices, etc. were an ongoing reminder that sinful people cannot have unhindered access to a holy God.

We know the end of the ultimate story where the curtain will be torn—but doesn't the anticipation excite you? Can't you see how each book builds on the other and how all of it thus far ties together? Let's keep reading!

IDEAS
FOR YOUR
REST DAY

Catch up on any missed reading.

Pause to study a text or chapter using your favorite Bible study method.

Identify a person or situation in the text, and learn more about their story.

Leviticus 1

to

Leviticus 24

	1 What do you learn about God and His character in these verses?
Consider	2 Where is Jesus in these chapters? Where do you see the gospel?
	3 How might you apply these verses to your life?

DAY 1 • *Read* Leviticus 1–5

BONUS QUESTION: When you see a law, even if it's confusing, consider asking yourself: In this season of their history, is this a law meant to help the people of Israel love God or love others? "I don't know" is a perfect answer; the goal is to think about how God's love fits into Jesus' summary, "love God, love your neighbor."

Say or write your prayer:

1 What do you learn about God and His character in these verses?
2 Where is Jesus in these chapters? Where do you see the gospel?
3 How might you apply these verses to your life?

DAY 2 • *Read* Leviticus 6–9

BONUS QUESTION: When you see a law, even if it's confusing, consider asking yourself: In this season of their history, is this a law meant to help the people of Israel love God or love others? "I don't know" is a perfect answer; the goal is to think about how God's love fits into Jesus' summary, "love God, love your neighbor."

Say or write your prayer:

Consider | 1 What do you learn about God and His character in these verses?
2 Where is Jesus in these chapters? Where do you see the gospel?
3 How might you apply these verses to your life?

DAY 3 • *Read* Leviticus 10–13

....

....

....

....

....

BONUS QUESTION: When you see a law, even if it's confusing, consider asking yourself: In this season of their history, is this a law meant to help the people of Israel love God or love others? "I don't know" is a perfect answer; the goal is to think about how God's love fits into Jesus' summary, "love God, love your neighbor."

....

....

....

Say or write your prayer:

1 What do you learn about God and His character in these verses?
2 Where is Jesus in these chapters? Where do you see the gospel?
3 How might you apply these verses to your life?

DAY 4 • *Read* Leviticus 14–16

BONUS QUESTION: When you see a law, even if it's confusing, consider asking yourself: In this season of their history, is this a law meant to help the people of Israel love God or love others? "I don't know" is a perfect answer; the goal is to think about how God's love fits into Jesus' summary, "love God, love your neighbor."

Say or write your prayer:

1 What do you learn about God and His character in these verses?
2 Where is Jesus in these chapters? Where do you see the gospel?
3 How might you apply these verses to your life?

DAY 5 • *Read* Leviticus 17–20

BONUS QUESTION: When you see a law, even if it's confusing, consider asking yourself: In this season of their history, is this a law meant to help the people of Israel love God or love others? "I don't know" is a perfect answer; the goal is to think about how God's love fits into Jesus' summary, "love God, love your neighbor."

Say or write your prayer:

1 What do you learn about God and His character in these verses?
2 Where is Jesus in these chapters? Where do you see the gospel?
3 How might you apply these verses to your life?

DAY 6 • *Read* Leviticus 21–24

BONUS QUESTION: When you see a law, even if it's confusing, consider asking yourself: In this season of their history, is this a law meant to help the people of Israel love God or love others? "I don't know" is a perfect answer; the goal is to think about how God's love fits into Jesus' summary, "love God, love your neighbor."

Say or write your prayer:

| *The Law*

You've made it to Leviticus, and you've read the first twenty-four chapters. Let's be honest, we are thrilled to be through it. Let's be honest again, we are grateful that we don't have to do most of those things. We see the psalmist singing, "Oh how I love your law" (Ps. 119:97), so why do we struggle to get through Leviticus? What are we missing?

The law helped the Israelites understand what to do to be in God's presence. It was a gift to them. As I thought about Leviticus, I thought about parenting. Admittedly, my analogy will fall short because I am not the Holy One (!), but stay with me.

As a loving parent, I have set out to shepherd my kids, and that includes certain rules and codes of conduct. My children believe I am their parent, they trust me as their parent (as much as humanly possible), and they submit to my rules. Now, none of these things make them more or less my children. Their obedience won't make them more mine or less mine. But their obedience does help maintain a healthy relationship. (This is another place where my analogy falls short; I can't imagine a severed relationship because of their disobedience, but of course, it's possible).

Leviticus has a context that helps us appreciate the book. The law set the people apart from other nations and those that followed ancient gods. It also shines a light on the holiness of God and all that is required to be in His presence. And that's when we say, yet again, thanks be to God, our Lord and Savior Jesus Christ.

IDEAS FOR YOUR REST DAY

Catch up on any missed reading.

Pause to study a text or chapter using your favorite Bible study method.

Identify a person or situation in the text, and learn more about their story.

Leviticus 25
to
Numbers 14

1 What do you learn about God and His character in these verses?
2 Where is Jesus in these chapters? Where do you see the gospel?
3 How might you apply these verses to your life?

DAY 1 • *Read* Leviticus 25–27

DAY 2 • *Read* Numbers 1–3

Say or write your prayer:

Consider

1 What do you learn about God and His character in these verses?
2 Where is Jesus in these chapters? Where do you see the gospel?
3 How might you apply these verses to your life?

DAY 3 • *Read* Numbers 4–6

DAY 4 • *Read* Numbers 7–8

Say or write your prayer:

1 What do you learn about God and His character in these verses?
2 Where is Jesus in these chapters? Where do you see the gospel?
3 How might you apply these verses to your life?

DAY 5 • *Read* Numbers 9–11

DAY 6 • *Read* Numbers 12–14

Say or write your prayer:

Is Numbers about More than Actual Numbers?

I n Hebrew the word for Numbers means "in the wilderness,"[1] which is significant because it's also where we find ourselves as we read Numbers (1:1). Imagine that we are sitting at Mount Sinai—in the place mentioned in Exodus and where we began in Leviticus. The setting of Numbers reminds me of Genesis 2. We know that in Genesis 1 God created humans; in Genesis 2, we get more details, and we grow to understand Adam and Eve's relationship to each other, the world, and God. Understanding the full picture helps us when we get to Genesis 3. Similarly, we gain a deeper understanding of two generations (thus the census) when we read the historical book of Numbers.

But I'd also like to draw your attention to Numbers 6:22–27. You are likely familiar with verses 24–26:

> The LORD bless you and keep you;
> the LORD make his face to shine upon you and be gracious
>   to you;
> the LORD lift up his countenance upon you and give you peace.

God's blessing on Israel has been repeated and sung for centuries. But the blessing's purpose and climax are rarely reflected on. In verse 27, the Lord says that His name would be upon His people. What a significant honor and privilege. God cared intimately for every person in every tribe.

BIBLE GENRES

The Bible includes books, and each book falls into a biblical genre. As author Kristie Anyabwile wrote: "The Bible is meant to be understood according to its literary genre. We say 'literary genre' because the Bible is an inspired work that uses conventional literary techniques to aid our understanding."[2]

LAW	Genesis, Exodus, Leviticus, Numbers, Deuteronomy
OLD TESTAMENT HISTORICAL NARRATIVE	Joshua, Judges, Ruth, 1 and 2 Samuel, 1 and 2 Kings, 1 and 2 Chronicles, Ezra, Nehemiah, Esther
PROPHETIC	Isaiah, Jeremiah, Ezekiel, Lamentations, Hosea, Joel, Amos, Obadiah, Jonah, Micah, Nahum, Habakkuk, Zephaniah, Haggai, Zechariah, Malachi
APOCALYPTIC	Daniel, Revelation
WISDOM	Job, Psalms, Proverbs, Ecclesiastes, Song of Solomon (many of the wisdom books are also poetry)
GOSPELS	Matthew, Mark, Luke, John
CHURCH HISTORY	Acts
PAULINE EPISTLES	Romans, 1 and 2 Corinthians, Galatians, Ephesians, Philippians, Colossians, 1 and 2 Thessalonians, 1 and 2 Timothy, Titus, Colossians, Philemon
GENERAL EPISTLES	Hebrews; James; 1 and 2 Peter; 1, 2, and 3 John; Jude

Catch up on any missed reading.

Pause to study a text or chapter using your favorite Bible study method.

Identify a person or situation in the text, and learn more about their story.

·

·

Numbers 15
to
Numbers 33

1 What do you learn about God and His character in these verses?

2 Where is Jesus in these chapters? Where do you see the gospel?

3 How might you apply these verses to your life?

DAY 1 • *Read* Numbers 15–17

DAY 2 • *Read* Numbers 18–20

Say or write your prayer:

1 What do you learn about God and His character in these verses?
2 Where is Jesus in these chapters? Where do you see the gospel?
3 How might you apply these verses to your life?

DAY 3 • *Read* Numbers 21–23

DAY 4 • *Read* Numbers 24–26

Say or write your prayer:

Consider

1 What do you learn about God and His character in these verses?
2 Where is Jesus in these chapters? Where do you see the gospel?
3 How might you apply these verses to your life?

DAY 5 • *Read* Numbers 27–30

DAY 6 • *Read* Numbers 31–33

Say or write your prayer:

Balaam—a Warning to the Wise

When was the last time you heard a teaching on the prophet Balaam? I don't recall anyone teaching me about him and about his cunning wickedness, but he played a significant role in the disobedience and faithlessness that we often refer to when we think of Old Testament Israel. You'll recall that in Numbers 22–24, King Balak and God gave opposing instructions to Balaam. Balak ordered Balaam to curse Israel and promised to pay him; God instructed Balaam not to curse them because they were blessed (Num. 22:10–12). So, although Balaam was not one of God's people, he followed God's instructions, and when Balaam spoke he proclaimed truth and real prophecies.

By the end of chapter 24, all seems well with the Israelites, but things quickly take a bad turn. By chapter 25, we read that the people of Israel were worshiping a false god and committing sexual immorality. God rightly punished them for these acts. But it isn't until chapter 31 that we learn that it was Balaam who advised the Moabites to entice Israel (Num. 31:16).

There's a lot we can learn from Balaam's story, but in an age where it can be hard to identify false teachers, maybe there are two messages and warnings for us today. As Jude proclaimed, "Woe to them! For they have gone the way of Cain, and for pay they have given themselves up to the error of Balaam, and perished in the rebellion of Korah" (Jude v. 11 NASB). It's hard to identify greedy false teachers, but we can ask the Lord for two things: 1) wisdom and discernment as we listen to others, and 2) protection from temptation and strength to resist the allure of sin.

IDEAS FOR YOUR REST DAY

Catch up on any missed reading.

Pause to study a text or chapter using your favorite Bible study method.

Identify a person or situation in the text, and learn more about their story.

HEAR, O ISRAEL:
THE LORD OUR
GOD, THE LORD
IS ONE. YOU
SHALL LOVE THE
LORD YOUR GOD
WITH ALL YOUR
HEART AND WITH
ALL YOUR SOUL
AND WITH ALL
YOUR MIGHT.

Numbers 34
to
Deuteronomy 19

1 What do you learn about God and His character in these verses?
2 Where is Jesus in these chapters? Where do you see the gospel?
3 How might you apply these verses to your life?

DAY 1 • *Read* Numbers 34–36

DAY 2 • *Read* Deuteronomy 1–3

Say or write your prayer:

Consider

1 What do you learn about God and His character in these verses?
2 Where is Jesus in these chapters? Where do you see the gospel?
3 How might you apply these verses to your life?

DAY 3 • *Read* Deuteronomy 4–6

DAY 4 • *Read* Deuteronomy 7–10

Say or write your prayer:

Consider

1 What do you learn about God and His character in these verses?
2 Where is Jesus in these chapters? Where do you see the gospel?
3 How might you apply these verses to your life?

DAY 5 • *Read* Deuteronomy 11–14

DAY 6 • *Read* Deuteronomy 15–19

Say or write your prayer:

Their Law Is Our Law

In the beginning of Deuteronomy, Moses warns the new generation of God's people to obey the law. Chapter 6 is likely one of the most significant chapters in Deuteronomy. It contains the attention-grabbing word "hear" (*shema*),[1] and it's quite familiar to us:

> "Hear, O Israel: The LORD our God, the LORD is one. You shall love the LORD your God with all your heart and with all your soul and with all your might." (Deut. 6:4–5)

The Shema was a daily prayer for ancient Israel.[2] It's important because the meaning is less about hearing and much more about doing. In other words, the people were commanded to obey the law and bind it on their hearts, meditate on it, and teach future generations (vv. 6–9). For us modern-day Christians, the command remains the same.

Jesus commands:

> "The most important is, 'Hear, O Israel: The Lord our God, the Lord is one. And you shall love the Lord your God with all your heart and with all your soul and with all your mind and with all your strength.' The second is this: 'You shall love your neighbor as yourself.' There is no other commandment greater than these." (Mark 12:29–31)

The entire law is summed up in these commands for us. We can't obey perfectly. Thanks be to God for His Son who forgives our imperfect obedience. And thanks be to God for the Holy Spirit who empowers us to obey.

IDEAS
FOR YOUR
REST DAY

Catch up on any missed reading.

Pause to study a text or chapter using your favorite Bible study method.

Identify a person or situation in the text, and learn more about their story.

Deuteronomy 20
to
Joshua 8

1 What do you learn about God and His character in these verses?
2 Where is Jesus in these chapters? Where do you see the gospel?
3 How might you apply these verses to your life?

DAY 1 • *Read* Deuteronomy 20–24

DAY 2 • *Read* Deuteronomy 25–28

Say or write your prayer:

1 What do you learn about God and His character in these verses?
2 Where is Jesus in these chapters? Where do you see the gospel?
3 How might you apply these verses to your life?

DAY 3 • *Read* Deuteronomy 29–31

DAY 4 • *Read* Deuteronomy 32–34

Say or write your prayer:

1 What do you learn about God and His character in these verses?
2 Where is Jesus in these chapters? Where do you see the gospel?
3 How might you apply these verses to your life?

DAY 5 • *Read* Joshua 1–4

DAY 6 • *Read* Joshua 5–8

Say or write your prayer:

Knowledge of God
vs. Knowing God

Abraham and Moses have been the primary leaders in the story of Scripture thus far. But after the death of Moses, God's people would need a new leader to take them into the promised land. Joshua is that leader. But in God's kindness to us, He told the story of Rahab, a Gentile and a prostitute. In my Bible study, *A Great Cloud of Witnesses*, I spend a week reflecting on the life of Rahab in the book of Joshua. In light of all our Bible reading and, Lord willing, accumulation of knowledge, I'm sharing an excerpt from my study.

J. I. Packer wrote in *Knowing God* that, "one can know a great deal about God without much knowledge of him."[1] Rahab knew a great deal about God and the history of Israel. Let's take a look at Joshua 2:9–11:

> I know that the LORD has given you the land, and that the fear of you has fallen upon us, and that all the inhabitants of the land melt away before you. For we have heard how the LORD dried up the water of the Red Sea before you when you came out of Egypt, and what you did to the two kings of the Amorites who were beyond the Jordan, to Sihon and Og, whom you devoted to destruction. And as soon as we heard it, our hearts melted, and there was no spirit left in any man because of you, for the LORD your God, he is God in the heavens above and on the earth beneath.

It's actually remarkable how much Rahab knew given her background and personal history. She had heard and paid attention. But more than that, she believed and trusted in God. Rahab knew more about God and His greatness than the spies could have imagined. Her knowledge led to worship and the fear of the Lord.

J. I. Packer warns that "if we pursue theological knowledge for its own sake, it is bound to go bad on us. It will make us proud and conceited."[2]

Although we do not know when Rahab came to believing faith, she not only understood God's covenant with Abraham and what would happen to Jericho, she spoke of God's greatness. But again, anyone could say these things—even demons know about the Lord and shudder (James 2:19). But her knowledge led her to faithful action. Her knowledge of God led her to act bravely and help the spies, and her trust in God led her to plead for her family (Josh. 2:12–14).[3]

Catch up on any missed reading.

Pause to study a text or chapter using your favorite Bible study method.

Identify a person or situation in the text, and learn more about their story.

Joshua 9
to
Judges 6

1 What do you learn about God and His character in these verses?

2 Where is Jesus in these chapters? Where do you see the gospel?

3 How might you apply these verses to your life?

DAY 1 • *Read* Joshua 9–12

DAY 2 • *Read* Joshua 13–17

Say or write your prayer:

1 What do you learn about God and His character in these verses?
2 Where is Jesus in these chapters? Where do you see the gospel?
3 How might you apply these verses to your life?

DAY 3 • *Read* Joshua 18–21

_____

_____

_____

_____

_____

DAY 4 • *Read* Joshua 22–24

_____

_____

_____

_____

_____

Say or write your prayer:

Consider

1 What do you learn about God and His character in these verses?
2 Where is Jesus in these chapters? Where do you see the gospel?
3 How might you apply these verses to your life?

DAY 5 • *Read* Judges 1–3

DAY 6 • *Read* Judges 4–6

Say or write your prayer:

His Ways Are Better

God's ways are not my ways. His ways are always good. His ways are better. His ways are pure. These are a few of the things I have to remind myself as I finish up reading through Joshua. The Canaanites were evil and their punishment was just. But I don't think that the Lord is calling me to fully understand. Rather, when we read through Joshua, I think the Lord is calling you and me to trust Him. The message at the end of Joshua is a call for Israel to fear the Lord and decide whom they will serve. God has been faithful. God had fulfilled His promises to them. Now, what are they going to do with that? (Josh. 24:14–18)

So, with the knowledge of God's character and faithfulness in our own lives, what are we going to do with that? Let's learn to trust Him even when we don't fully understand and fear Him.

IDEAS FOR YOUR REST DAY

Catch up on any missed reading.

Pause to study a text or chapter using your favorite Bible study method.

Identify a person or situation in the text, and learn more about their story.

A Quick Look at the Storyline
of the Old Testament

Although our Week 10 reflection is in Joshua, our reading is right at the beginning of Judges. As we continue our journey through the history of Israel, here's a simple outline of where we've been and where we are going.[1]

Creation

Patriarchs

Moses and Exodus

Conquest

Judges

United Kingdom

Divided Kingdom

Exile

Return

"Silence"[2]

Judges 7
to
Ruth 4

1 What do you learn about God and His character in these verses?

2 Where is Jesus in these chapters? Where do you see the gospel?

3 How might you apply these verses to your life?

DAY 1 • *Read* Judges 7–9

DAY 2 • *Read* Judges 10–13

Say or write your prayer:

1 What do you learn about God and His character in these verses?
2 Where is Jesus in these chapters? Where do you see the gospel?
3 How might you apply these verses to your life?

DAY 3 • *Read* Judges 14–16

DAY 4 • *Read* Judges 17–19

Say or write your prayer:

1 What do you learn about God and His character in these verses?
2 Where is Jesus in these chapters? Where do you see the gospel?
3 How might you apply these verses to your life?

DAY 5 • *Read* Judges 20–21

DAY 6 • *Read* Ruth 1–4

Say or write your prayer:

An Unlikely Hero

Israel had gone her own way and was no longer following the Lord's commands. The Lord kept providing, but the people continually turned away. God raised up judges to lead them, but they didn't listen to these leaders (Judg. 2:16–19). In the midst of grievous stories of disobedience and apostasy is the story of the prophetess and judge, Deborah. You met her in our Week 10 reading, and her life and practice stand in sharp contrast to Israel's other leaders, such as Jephthah, Samson, and the Levite. The book ends horribly, but Deborah is a bright spot worth the attention.

Deborah stood out among the judges. Besides the obvious—she was a woman—she would have stood out also because of her godliness. She feared the Lord. Barak, another judge, respected her, so much so that he refused to go into battle unless she joined him (Judg. 4:6–8). Take note too that he went to battle after she reminded him of the Lord's command and instructed him to do so. Deborah doesn't take the credit and instead sings a song of praise to the Lord (chapter 5).

Deborah is an example of strength, resolve, wisdom, obedience, and humility. No wonder many mention her as a leader to emulate.

IDEAS FOR YOUR REST DAY

Catch up on any missed reading.

Pause to study a text or chapter using your favorite Bible study method.

Identify a person or situation in the text, and learn more about their story.

There was a certain man of zophim of the hill count whose name was Elkana Jeroham, son of Elihu, so son of Zuph, an Ephrath two wives. The name of Hannah, and the name of Peninnah. And Peninna but Hannah had no chil man used to go up year his city to worship and the LORD of hosts at Sh two sons of Eli, Hophni were priests of the LOR when Elkanah sacrificed

1 Samuel 1

to

1 Samuel 20

1 What do you learn about God and His character in these verses?
2 Where is Jesus in these chapters? Where do you see the gospel?
3 How might you apply these verses to your life?

DAY 1 • *Read* 1 Samuel 1–3

DAY 2 • *Read* 1 Samuel 4–8

Say or write your prayer:

1 What do you learn about God and His character in these verses?
2 Where is Jesus in these chapters? Where do you see the gospel?
3 How might you apply these verses to your life?

DAY 3 • *Read* 1 Samuel 9–11

DAY 4 • *Read* 1 Samuel 12–14

Say or write your prayer:

1 What do you learn about God and His character in these verses?

2 Where is Jesus in these chapters? Where do you see the gospel?

3 How might you apply these verses to your life?

DAY 5 • *Read* 1 Samuel 15–17

DAY 6 • *Read* 1 Samuel 18–20

Say or write your prayer:

Come to Him All Who Are Weary

We are well past the first chapter of Samuel, but I can't help but send us back to the beginning. Hannah was the wife of Elkanah, and she was barren. Unfortunately, Elkanah had another wife named Peninnah, who made Hannah's life miserable. Hannah was so miserable that at times she couldn't eat. Hannah longed for a child. We know the end of the story. Hannah gives birth to Samuel, Samuel becomes a judge and priest, and he appoints David as king of Israel. It's an amazing story that points to God's awesome providence.

But it's Hannah's humility that stands out to me. She didn't hide her anguish from the Lord or from anyone else. She cried out to Him. She pleaded with the Lord. She spoke out of anxiety and vexation (1 Sam. 1:16). We don't go to the Lord knowing how He will answer our prayers; but if we can learn one thing from Hannah, may it be that we can go to the Lord in our pain, confusion, sorrow, anxiety, and anguish. We don't have to go buttoned up. We can go to the Lord as we are, and my guess is that we will come away much more like Him.

IDEAS
FOR YOUR
REST DAY

Catch up on any missed reading.

Pause to study a text or chapter using your favorite Bible study method.

Identify a person or situation in the text, and learn more about their story.

1 Samuel 21
to
2 Samuel 11

1 What do you learn about God and His character in these verses?
2 Where is Jesus in these chapters? Where do you see the gospel?
3 How might you apply these verses to your life?

DAY 1 • *Read* 1 Samuel 21–23

DAY 2 • *Read* 1 Samuel 24–26

Say or write your prayer:

1 What do you learn about God and His character in these verses?
2 Where is Jesus in these chapters? Where do you see the gospel?
3 How might you apply these verses to your life?

DAY 3 • *Read* 1 Samuel 27–31

DAY 4 • *Read* 2 Samuel 1–3

Say or write your prayer:

1 What do you learn about God and His character in these verses?

2 Where is Jesus in these chapters? Where do you see the gospel?

3 How might you apply these verses to your life?

DAY 5 • *Read* 2 Samuel 4–7

DAY 6 • *Read* 2 Samuel 8–11

Say or write your prayer:

A Covenant with David

L et's look again at two verses from the reading from Day 5:

> "When your days are fulfilled and you lie down with your fathers, I will raise up your offspring after you, who shall come from your body, and I will establish his kingdom. He shall build a house for my name, and I will establish the throne of his kingdom forever." (2 Sam. 7:12–13)

David wanted to build a house for the Lord, but the Lord had better plans. God's plans are always better. Although this covenant is with David, the promise is truly for all nations. The Lord promised David that after he died, God would raise up someone from David's lineage to build God's house and establish His throne forever. The One who would establish God's throne *forever* is, of course, Jesus. But Solomon was David's offspring who was raised up after his death. In verse 14, we see a clue that God isn't referring to Solomon when He talks about a forever kingdom. God says: "When he commits iniquity..." Solomon had a kingdom, but not one that lasted forever. Solomon also sinned and disqualified himself and couldn't have been the one to fulfill this ultimate promise (1 Kings 11:1–2). Only the Messiah could do that.

God never once breaks His promises. He is a covenant-keeping God. No one could fulfill this promise except for His own Son.

> "He will be great and will be called the Son of the Most High. And the Lord God will give to him the throne of his father David, and he will reign over the house of Jacob forever, and of his kingdom there will be no end." (Luke 1:32–33)

And...

> "For our sake he made him to be sin who knew no sin, so that in him we might become the righteousness of God." (2 Cor. 5:21)

ENJOY YOUR REST DAY!

2 Samuel 12
to
1 Kings 2

1 What do you learn about God and His character in these verses?

2 Where is Jesus in these chapters? Where do you see the gospel?

3 How might you apply these verses to your life?

DAY 1 • *Read* 2 Samuel 12–14

DAY 2 • *Read* 2 Samuel 15–17

Say or write your prayer:

1 What do you learn about God and His character in these verses?
2 Where is Jesus in these chapters? Where do you see the gospel?
3 How might you apply these verses to your life?

DAY 3 • *Read* 2 Samuel 18–19

DAY 4 • *Read* 2 Samuel 20–22

Say or write your prayer:

1 What do you learn about God and His character in these verses?
2 Where is Jesus in these chapters? Where do you see the gospel?
3 How might you apply these verses to your life?

DAY 5 • *Read* 2 Samuel 23–24

DAY 6 • *Read* 1 Kings 1–2

Say or write your prayer:

Perfectly Just and Wholly Merciful

I won't rehash King David's sin; we know what happened and we know that it was all evil. We never want to make light of his abuse of power or act as if it wasn't as terrible as it was. When I read the Bible, look at the modern-day church, and even think about my own faults, it's clear to see that there are no heroes. Only God is the hero in the Bible and in our lives. It's a lesson that is hard to swallow. We all like a good story. David's sin has been minimized into a nice children's story of a man after God's own heart who did some bad things but is still the hero. It's not the way the Bible tells his story.

However, it's also true that only God would be so merciful to such a dreadful sinner. I'd likely bring up David's sin to him over and over again. I surely wouldn't allow his lineage to lead to the Savior of the world. David's sin didn't go unpunished; his life and his family's lives were in shambles and many rose up against him. Bottom line: there were consequences for his sin. But his sins were forgiven. Aren't we glad that God is the hero of the story? Aren't we glad that God is not like us? God is perfectly just and wholly merciful.

There are many who might read the story of David and find themselves concerned that the Lord overlooks abuse. A just God could never turn a blind eye on injustice. Every person will give an account for what they have done (Rom. 14:12). Although our shepherds may fail us, the Good Shepherd never will (John 10).

**IDEAS
FOR YOUR
REST DAY**

Catch up on any missed reading.

Pause to study a text or chapter using your favorite Bible study method.

Identify a person or situation in the text, and learn more about their story.

1 Kings 3
to
1 Kings 20

1 What do you learn about God and His character in these verses?
2 Where is Jesus in these chapters? Where do you see the gospel?
3 How might you apply these verses to your life?

DAY 1 • *Read* 1 Kings 3–6

DAY 2 • *Read* 1 Kings 7–8

Say or write your prayer:

1 What do you learn about God and His character in these verses?
2 Where is Jesus in these chapters? Where do you see the gospel?
3 How might you apply these verses to your life?

DAY 3 • *Read* 1 Kings 9–11

DAY 4 • *Read* 1 Kings 12–14

Say or write your prayer:

1 What do you learn about God and His character in these verses?

2 Where is Jesus in these chapters? Where do you see the gospel?

3 How might you apply these verses to your life?

DAY 5 • *Read* 1 Kings 15–17

DAY 6 • *Read* 1 Kings 18–20

Say or write your prayer:

Solomon's Wisdom, God's Mercy

S olomon is known for his wisdom, but it's the means by which God decided to display it and declare it to Israel that is striking. If you remember, in 1 Kings 3:16–28, two prostitutes came before the king because one of them stole the other prostitute's newborn baby. The women lived together and had babies at the same time. Unfortunately, one of the babies died during the night. The mother whose baby died switched the babies in the middle of the night and pretended to be his mother. Because of the law and the lack of witnesses, the two women were able to take their case before Solomon (Deut. 19:15).

Although these are very different stories and situations, I couldn't help but think about the story of another prostitute, Rahab, and the dignity and respect the two spies had for her (Josh. 2:8–14). Did Solomon have to take their case? Could he have treated them poorly instead of considering it? As I marveled at this story, I was reminded of a commentary I read on these verses:

> Like most cities of the world, African cities and towns have prostitutes. We tend to leave them to the mercy of those who use them to satisfy their evil sexual cravings and of the police who arrest them from time to time. Yet in God's program, they are as important as any other citizen.[1]

The text is meant to highlight the wisdom of Solomon, but I see the mercy of God. Time and time again, He bestows dignity on those whom we would shun. Because they're prostitutes, this story may not even have made our modern-day nightly news. But God uses their case to establish Solomon's wisdom and provide justice for a prostitute and her baby. Amazing grace.

IDEAS FOR YOUR REST DAY

Catch up on any missed reading.

Pause to study a text or chapter using your favorite Bible study method.

Identify a person or situation in the text, and learn more about their story.

Now Naboth the Jezree[l]

vineyard in Jezreel, besi[de]

of Ahab king of Samari[a]

this Ahab said to Nabot[h]

your vineyard, that I ma[y]

a vegetable garden, beca[use]

my house, and I will giv[e]

vineyard for it; or, if it se[em]

you, I will give you its va[lue]

But Naboth said to Aha[b]

forbid that I should give

inheritance of my fathe[r]

went into his house vex[ed]

because of what Nabot[h]

had said to him, for he [had]

1 Kings 21

to

2 Kings 15

1 What do you learn about God and His character in these verses?
2 Where is Jesus in these chapters? Where do you see the gospel?
3 How might you apply these verses to your life?

DAY 1 • *Read* 1 Kings 21–22

DAY 2 • *Read* 2 Kings 1–3

Say or write your prayer:

1 What do you learn about God and His character in these verses?
2 Where is Jesus in these chapters? Where do you see the gospel?
3 How might you apply these verses to your life?

DAY 3 • *Read* 2 Kings 4–6

DAY 4 • *Read* 2 Kings 7–9

Say or write your prayer:

1 What do you learn about God and His character in these verses?
2 Where is Jesus in these chapters? Where do you see the gospel?
3 How might you apply these verses to your life?

DAY 5 • *Read* 2 Kings 10–12

DAY 6 • *Read* 2 Kings 13–15

Say or write your prayer:

Lessons from Ahab's Repentance

Israel's history goes from bad to worse to downright depressing. The kings are evil, the people worship idols, and although we aren't there yet, soon Israel will be defeated by Babylon and exiled. What can we glean from such a doomsday book? Quite a bit! For example, can you believe that Ahab repented? Ahab's evil knew no bounds. His unfortunate eulogy could have been summed up as, "There was none who sold himself to do what was evil in the sight of the LORD like Ahab, whom Jezebel his wife incited" (1 Kings 21:25).

He was evil, and yet he repented (v. 27). Four things come to mind as I read this episode in 1 Kings: 1) No one is too far gone and out of the reach of God. 2) God is merciful; He forgives all who repent. 3) There are consequences to sin. Ahab's descendants bore the punishment prophesied by Elijah (2 Kings 10), and eventually, Ahab died in battle (1 Kings 22:34–35). 4) God is a just God.

God always has something to say in His Word.

IDEAS
FOR YOUR
REST DAY

Catch up on any missed reading.

Pause to study a text or chapter using your favorite Bible study method.

Identify a person or situation in the text, and learn more about their story.

2 Kings 16
to
1 Chronicles 9

Consider | 1 What do you learn about God and His character in these verses?
2 Where is Jesus in these chapters? Where do you see the gospel?
3 How might you apply these verses to your life?

DAY 1 • *Read* 2 Kings 16–18

DAY 2 • *Read* 2 Kings 19–21

Say or write your prayer:

1 What do you learn about God and His character in these verses?
2 Where is Jesus in these chapters? Where do you see the gospel?
3 How might you apply these verses to your life?

DAY 3 • *Read* 2 Kings 22–23

DAY 4 • *Read* 2 Kings 24–25

Say or write your prayer:

Consider

1 What do you learn about God and His character in these verses?
2 Where is Jesus in these chapters? Where do you see the gospel?
3 How might you apply these verses to your life?

DAY 5 • *Read* 1 Chronicles 1–5

DAY 6 • *Read* 1 Chronicles 6–9

Say or write your prayer:

Let's Study 2 Kings 22

To break up the density of our reading this week, let's pause and study. If you need to catch up on your reading, feel free to skip this reflection and keep reading instead. Grab a piece of paper or write in the space provided on your Rest Day.

Turn to 2 Kings 22. Using a basic Bible study method, you are going to:

1. Read the chapter.

2. Observe: ask questions like who, what, when, where, why, and how. Write out your answers.

3. Interpret: What does the text mean? What's the context? How does it relate to the rest of Scripture? Write out your answers.

4. Apply: Is there context for me today? Write out your answer and pray for the Lord's help to apply what you have learned.

5. I always make sure to ask: What does the text say about the character of God and/or how does it point to Jesus? Write out your answer.

As Josiah's kingdom was transformed by the discovery of the Book of the Law (2 Kings 22), I pray you will experience joy and transformation in your discoveries in God's Word.

I hope that you enjoyed this brief break to study. Feel free to use this method anytime you'd like to dig a little deeper during your reading time.

IDEAS FOR YOUR REST DAY

Catch up on any missed reading.

Pause to study a text or chapter using your favorite Bible study method.

Identify a person or situation in the text, and learn more about their story.

Bonus Idea: Work on your Week 17 Reflection Bible study on 2 Kings 22.

1 Chronicles 10

to

2 Chronicles 5

Consider	1 What do you learn about God and His character in these verses?
	2 Where is Jesus in these chapters? Where do you see the gospel?
	3 How might you apply these verses to your life?

DAY 1 • *Read* 1 Chronicles 10–14

DAY 2 • *Read* 1 Chronicles 15–17

Say or write your prayer:

1 What do you learn about God and His character in these verses?
2 Where is Jesus in these chapters? Where do you see the gospel?
3 How might you apply these verses to your life?

DAY 3 • *Read* 1 Chronicles 18–22

DAY 4 • *Read* 1 Chronicles 23–26

Say or write your prayer:

1 What do you learn about God and His character in these verses?

2 Where is Jesus in these chapters? Where do you see the gospel?

3 How might you apply these verses to your life?

DAY 5 • *Read* 1 Chronicles 27–29

DAY 6 • *Read* 2 Chronicles 1–5

Say or write your prayer:

What's in a Genealogy?

The older I get the more that I am intrigued by genealogies. I'd go so far as to say that I'm obsessed with genealogies. Part of my obsession may be that I can't trace my family centuries back. I see the importance and value in knowing one's family background. Genealogies aren't simply a list of names within one's ancestry, although they are certainly that. A genealogy is a map, a historical reference, a guide to understanding a person and events. So, let's just say I geek out in 1 Chronicles. For those who don't geek out about genealogies, most of us love a good story. Recently, I discovered that one of my husband's ancestors saved people from a railway catastrophe in England. Maybe you've found out something that's been surprising. Regardless, the stories of the past shape us today.

The Chronicler (author unknown) spends the first nine chapters on genealogies. However tempting it may be to skip, knowing how much people shape history, it's important to stop and read. Both 1 and 2 Chronicles map out the history of Israel and retrace events found in 1 and 2 Samuel and 1 and 2 Kings. If you can grasp the genealogies in the Bible, you can gain a better understanding of the history of Israel, the story of the Bible, and ultimately, the history of salvation.

IDEAS FOR YOUR REST DAY

Catch up on any missed reading.

Pause to study a text or chapter using your favorite Bible study method.

Identify a person or situation in the text, and learn more about their story.

2 Chronicles 6
to
2 Chronicles 33

1 What do you learn about God and His character in these verses?
2 Where is Jesus in these chapters? Where do you see the gospel?
3 How might you apply these verses to your life?

DAY 1 • *Read* 2 Chronicles 6–9

DAY 2 • *Read* 2 Chronicles 10–15

Say or write your prayer:

	1 What do you learn about God and His character in these verses?
Consider	2 Where is Jesus in these chapters? Where do you see the gospel?
	3 How might you apply these verses to your life?

DAY 3 • *Read* 2 Chronicles 16–20

_____

_____

_____

_____

_____

_____

DAY 4 • *Read* 2 Chronicles 21–25

_____

_____

_____

_____

_____

_____

Say or write your prayer:

1 What do you learn about God and His character in these verses?
2 Where is Jesus in these chapters? Where do you see the gospel?
3 How might you apply these verses to your life?

DAY 5 • *Read* 2 Chronicles 26–29

DAY 6 • *Read* 2 Chronicles 30–33

Say or write your prayer:

Seek and He Shall Be Found

Reread this verse from the Day 1 reading:

"If my people who are called by my name humble themselves, and pray and seek my face and turn from their wicked ways, then I will hear from heaven and will forgive their sin and heal their land." (2 Chron. 7:14)

After Solomon dedicated the temple, God answered Solomon's prayer with promises, but these promises were contingent on the humility and obedience of His people. God is a covenant-keeping God, but His name cannot be trampled on. God desires for Israel to submit to His law and seek His face. What a glorious invitation! Although there is a specific time, place, and context for these verses (e.g., God has not made a covenant with my country or your country), throughout the Scriptures, we see this same invitation for all of God's people. Through His Son, God has provided a way for us to humble ourselves, approach His throne of grace, and receive His favor. Just like for the Israelites, there is freedom, grace, and joy when we submit our lives to Him:

"Ask, and it will be given to you; seek, and you will find; knock, and it will be opened to you." (Matt. 7:7)

IDEAS
FOR YOUR
REST DAY

Catch up on any missed reading.

Pause to study a text or chapter using your favorite Bible study method.

Identify a person or situation in the text, and learn more about their story.

Josiah was eight years o[ld when he]
began to reign, and he r[eigned thirty-]
one years in Jerusalem. [And he]
was right in the eyes of [the LORD, and]
walked in the ways of D[avid]
and he did not turn asid[e to the right]
hand or to the left. For i[n the eighth]
year of his reign, while h[e was yet a]
boy, he began to seek th[e God of David]
his father, and in the tw[elfth year he]
began to purge Judah an[d Jerusalem of]
the high places, the Ash[erim, and the]
carved and the metal im[ages. And they]
chopped down the altar[s of the Baals]
in his presence, and he

2 Chronicles 34
to
Nehemiah 9

1 What do you learn about God and His character in these verses?
2 Where is Jesus in these chapters? Where do you see the gospel?
3 How might you apply these verses to your life?

DAY 1 · *Read* 2 Chronicles 34–36

DAY 2 · *Read* Ezra 1–4

Say or write your prayer:

1 What do you learn about God and His character in these verses?
2 Where is Jesus in these chapters? Where do you see the gospel?
3 How might you apply these verses to your life?

DAY 3 • *Read* Ezra 5–7

DAY 4 • *Read* Ezra 8–10

Say or write your prayer:

1 What do you learn about God and His character in these verses?
2 Where is Jesus in these chapters? Where do you see the gospel?
3 How might you apply these verses to your life?

DAY 5 • *Read* Nehemiah 1–5

DAY 6 • *Read* Nehemiah 6–9

Say or write your prayer:

Ezra and Context

Most of you, like me, are average Bible readers—you likely aren't fluent in Hebrew and Greek. Some of you may be new to the Bible or have some basic knowledge. You love Jesus and want to know Him. So, spending days and weeks at a time in the historical books of the Bible may feel like a chore. As I was thinking about how the books of the Bible connect to one another and the purpose and importance of these historical books, I came across a helpful paragraph in the *Moody Bible Commentary* that summarizes my general thoughts and helps motivate me to keep reading.

> [The book of] Ezra contributes to the biblical narrative in four ways. (1) It provides the narrative description of the return of the Judeans from the Babylonian captivity and thus continues the story that began in 1 and 2 Chronicles. . . . (3) It provides the historical context for the prophetic ministries of Haggai and Zechariah; without Ezra their prophetic oracles would lack significant context.[1]

Although the writer is focused on the book of Ezra, the general idea could be applied to everything you've read over the past twenty weeks. The Pentateuch (the first five books of the Bible) and most of the historical books lay the foundation and context for the books that follow them. The stories also show us that God had relationships with real fallen humans who He invited into His covenant. God delights in working through limited humans!

We are now close to the halfway mark of our yearlong reading. If you need additional help understanding what you're reading, consider using one of your Rest Days to read a few paragraphs of a study Bible or commentary. These tools can help you understand the context as we finish up and head into the wisdom and poetry literary genres of the Bible.

ENJOY YOUR REST DAY!

Nehemiah 10
to
Job 15

1 What do you learn about God and His character in these verses?
2 Where is Jesus in these chapters? Where do you see the gospel?
3 How might you apply these verses to your life?

DAY 1 • *Read* Nehemiah 10–13

DAY 2 • *Read* Esther 1–5

Say or write your prayer:

1 What do you learn about God and His character in these verses?
2 Where is Jesus in these chapters? Where do you see the gospel?
3 How might you apply these verses to your life?

DAY 3 • _Read_ Esther 6–10

DAY 4 • _Read_ Job 1–5

Say or write your prayer:

1 What do you learn about God and His character in these verses?
2 Where is Jesus in these chapters? Where do you see the gospel?
3 How might you apply these verses to your life?

DAY 5 • *Read* Job 6–10

DAY 6 • *Read* Job 11–15

Say or write your prayer:

An Unusual Yet Relatable Story

Job's story seems unreal. Everything was taken from him—his wealth, his family, and every tangible good thing. Could this really have happened to a person? Is it just an allegory or a lesson? But then I think of a recent tornado that swept through a town, taking with it property and life. Or the destructive power of a bomb killing young children and causing others to flee and leave behind everything they ever knew, including their homeland. Or my grandmother, who outlived her mom, dad, brothers and sisters, husband, and two sons. Her loss wasn't sudden, but was slow and excruciating. Now, Job's story doesn't seem so unlikely.

The book of Job doesn't give us a clear answer for his sufferings. We know that Job was a righteous man who feared the Lord (Job 1:1). We know that Job's friends weren't a great comfort to him (Job 21:34). We know that Job was anguished by his troubles. What is the point of this book? I won't spoil the next devotional or the end of his book. However, I will say that some of the answers we desire we may not get. Job's story and the story of countless others, including my own, reminds me of lyrics from William Cowper's hymn, "God Moves in a Mysterious Way":

> *His purposes will ripen fast,*
> *Unfolding ev'ry hour;*
> *The bud may have a bitter taste,*
> *But sweet will be the flow'r.*[1]

There will be moments in our lives when the bud of whatever is happening has a bitter taste. We can't know all of God's purposes, but we can learn to lean on Him and trust Him more every hour. In the unknown and confusing days, I rest in the unchanging, all-powerful God. Perhaps learning to trust the Lord is one of the things God wants us to glean from reading Job.

ENJOY YOUR REST DAY!

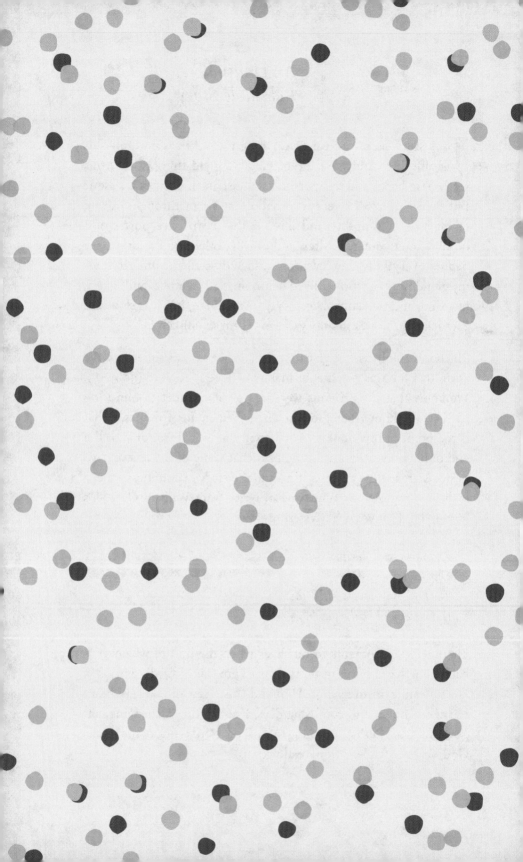

Job 16
to
Psalm 8

1 What do you learn about God and His character in these verses?

2 Where is Jesus in these chapters? Where do you see the gospel?

3 How might you apply these verses to your life?

DAY 1 • *Read* Job 16–21

DAY 2 • *Read* Job 22–28

Say or write your prayer:

1 What do you learn about God and His character in these verses?
2 Where is Jesus in these chapters? Where do you see the gospel?
3 How might you apply these verses to your life?

DAY 3 • *Read* Job 29–32

DAY 4 • *Read* Job 33–37

Say or write your prayer:

1 What do you learn about God and His character in these verses?
2 Where is Jesus in these chapters? Where do you see the gospel?
3 How might you apply these verses to your life?

DAY 5 • *Read* Job 38–42

DAY 6 • *Read* Psalms 1–8

Say or write your prayer:

Not Promised for All

Job's story is inspiring and is often used to highlight perseverance through suffering. But Job's story ends in restoration. Let's reread God's Word:

> And the LORD restored the fortunes of Job, when he had prayed for his friends. And the LORD gave Job twice as much as he had before. Then came to him all his brothers and sisters and all who had known him before, and ate bread with him in his house. And they showed him sympathy and comforted him for all the evil that the LORD had brought upon him. And each of them gave him a piece of money and a ring of gold. (Job 42:10–11)

The text continues by saying that the Lord blessed Job's later days of his life more than the beginning. He died an old man with a full life (v. 17). I have experienced four miscarriages. I had two miscarriages and then gave birth to my son. I had two more miscarriages and then gave birth to my daughter. Although I would never wish to have experienced that loss and pain over again, I also can't imagine not having the kids the Lord has allowed me to raise. In some ways, there was restoration. My earthly kids didn't replace my kids that didn't live, but they are a gift that I wouldn't trade for anything. I imagine Job might have felt similarly. Life can be paradoxical at times, can't it?

I wonder if the idea of faith in God and trusting in the sovereign hand of God is only comforting when we think He will restore us. The Lord never promises restoration of all things during our lifetime. For example, I have chronic pain and stomach issues related to one of my miscarriages. But we can trust that He will redeem our situations. We can trust that He is doing something good. It's when we truly understand God's character that we can say, "Blessed be the name of the LORD" (Job 1:21).

ENJOY YOUR REST DAY!

Psalm 9
to
Psalm 40

Consider | 1 What do you learn about God and His character in these verses?
2 Where is Jesus in these chapters? Where do you see the gospel?
3 How might you apply these verses to your life?

DAY 1 • *Read* Psalms 9–15

DAY 2 • *Read* Psalms 16–19

Say or write your prayer:

1 What do you learn about God and His character in these verses?
2 Where is Jesus in these chapters? Where do you see the gospel?
3 How might you apply these verses to your life?

DAY 3 • *Read* Psalms 20–26

DAY 4 • *Read* Psalms 27–32

Say or write your prayer:

Consider

1 What do you learn about God and His character in these verses?
2 Where is Jesus in these chapters? Where do you see the gospel?
3 How might you apply these verses to your life?

DAY 5 • *Read* Psalms 33–36

DAY 6 • *Read* Psalms 37–40

Say or write your prayer:

#Blessed

By this time, you've read forty psalms. The Psalms are rich with lament and rejoicing, sorrow and joy, singing and crying. It's here that we get a sense that there's permission to feel however we feel and bring it to the Lord. Although we are long past Psalm 1, I wanted us to reflect on the beginning of our journey through these songs and poems.

We all want to be blessed. We desire happiness. Here's a prescription for happiness from Psalm 1:1 that you won't see at your local pharmacy: "Don't walk with the wicked!" But Psalm 1 also leads us toward true happiness, toward a life lived delighting in the law of the Lord and meditating on it day and night. Perhaps I should have started this book with that message. You want a blessed life? Read your Bible. Ask the Lord to help you meditate on His Word.

This is likely a great time to remind you that if you haven't read the assigned book in your reading list, and find yourself skipping around, that is not only okay, it's wonderful! You are reading the Bible. My hope for you and me is that we would delight in the law of the Lord and ultimately be led to a knowledge of and love for our Savior. The goal isn't to check off a list; it's to delight. Lord, make it so.

IDEAS FOR YOUR REST DAY	Catch up on any missed reading.
	Pause to study a text or chapter using your favorite Bible study method.
	Identify a person or situation in the text, and learn more about their story.

Blessed is the one who c

In the day of trouble the

the LORD protects him

he is called blessed in

you do not give him u

The LORD sustains him

in his illness you resto

As for me, I said, "O LO

heal me, for I have sin

My enemies say of me in

"When will he die, and

And when one comes to

while his heart gathers

when he goes out, he

All who hate me whispe

Psalm 41
to
Psalm 77

1 What do you learn about God and His character in these verses?
2 Where is Jesus in these chapters? Where do you see the gospel?
3 How might you apply these verses to your life?

DAY 1 • *Read* Psalms 41–46

DAY 2 • *Read* Psalms 47–53

Say or write your prayer:

1 What do you learn about God and His character in these verses?
2 Where is Jesus in these chapters? Where do you see the gospel?
3 How might you apply these verses to your life?

DAY 3 • *Read* Psalms 54–60

DAY 4 • *Read* Psalms 61–68

Say or write your prayer:

Consider	1 What do you learn about God and His character in these verses?
	2 Where is Jesus in these chapters? Where do you see the gospel?
	3 How might you apply these verses to your life?

DAY 5 • *Read* Psalms 69–72

DAY 6 • *Read* Psalms 73–77

Say or write your prayer:

Learning to Lament

People have varying opinions about personality tests, so I'll refrain from sharing my "personality," but let's just say, I don't like to lament. I want to be happy and escape from any feelings of longing. I don't like the idea of sitting with my feelings. No thanks! However, through a series of devastating circumstances, I've learned that lamentation is not only appropriate, it's healthy. As I've suffered and grown in my understanding of lament, much of what I've learned has stemmed from reading the Psalms, while also learning about the life of Jesus through the Gospels.

Psalm 42 (along with Psalm 43) is an example of the type of honest, vulnerable, and lamenting language God invites us to share with Him. In the case of this psalm, it would appear that the psalmist wrote it to be sung congregationally (see the heading before verse 1). He longed for the presence of the Lord and acknowledged his deep sorrow as he waited (vv. 1–3). In the past, in a season of spiritual depression and sadness, I might have said to my soul, "Suck it up." But not the psalmist. He doesn't rely on his own strength and might. Instead, he turns to God: "Hope in God; for I shall again praise him, my salvation and my God" (vv. 5b–6).

The next time you sense sorrow, remember that it isn't a sign of weakness; even Jesus was sorrowful (Isa. 53:3; Matt. 26:38). Rather, it is a sign of our humanity and our need for our Rock and Salvation. The Psalms remind us that we can take every pain, confusion, and sadness straight to the Lord—they remind us where our help comes from.

IDEAS
FOR YOUR
REST DAY

Catch up on any missed reading.

Pause to study a text or chapter using your favorite Bible study method.

Identify a person or situation in the text, and learn more about their story.

WEEK 25

Psalm 78
to
Psalm 118

1 What do you learn about God and His character in these verses?
2 Where is Jesus in these chapters? Where do you see the gospel?
3 How might you apply these verses to your life?

DAY 1 • *Read* Psalms 78–82

DAY 2 • *Read* Psalms 83–89

Say or write your prayer:

1 What do you learn about God and His character in these verses?
2 Where is Jesus in these chapters? Where do you see the gospel?
3 How might you apply these verses to your life?

DAY 3 • *Read* Psalms 90–99

DAY 4 • *Read* Psalms 100–105

Say or write your prayer:

Consider | 1 What do you learn about God and His character in these verses?
2 Where is Jesus in these chapters? Where do you see the gospel?
3 How might you apply these verses to your life?

DAY 5 • *Read* Psalms 106–109

DAY 6 • *Read* Psalms 110–118

Say or write your prayer:

Shout for Joy!

I love the image of entering the presence of the Lord with singing in Psalm 100. There's much to be grateful for, but as I read, I got stuck on verse 3: "Know that the LORD, he is God! It is he who made us, and we are his; we are his people, and the sheep of his pasture."

He made us and we are His. There's something comforting in knowing that we aren't only created by God but there's Kingship. But He is not only King; He is our Shepherd. We are His sheep and He shepherds us. A shepherd guides and protects. Not one of His sheep is unaccounted for. And so, we rejoice! Thank you, Lord, for making us and taking care of us. Thank you for being unashamed to associate with us and call us your own. We are yours. Thank you!

IDEAS FOR YOUR REST DAY

Catch up on any missed reading.

Pause to study a text or chapter using your favorite Bible study method.

Identify a person or situation in the text, and learn more about their story.

Psalm 119

to

Proverbs 8

1 What do you learn about God and His character in these verses?
2 Where is Jesus in these chapters? Where do you see the gospel?
3 How might you apply these verses to your life?

DAY 1 • *Read* Psalms 119

DAY 2 • *Read* Psalms 120–135

Say or write your prayer:

DAY 3 • *Read* Psalms 136–143

DAY 4 • *Read* Psalms 144–150

Say or write your prayer:

1 What do you learn about God and His character in these verses?
2 Where is Jesus in these chapters? Where do you see the gospel?
3 How might you apply these verses to your life?

DAY 5 • *Read* Proverbs 1–4

DAY 6 • *Read* Proverbs 5–8

Say or write your prayer:

Fear Before Wisdom and Knowledge

We've finished the Psalms and entered a book filled with wisdom. Or perhaps I should say another book filled with wisdom, since the Psalms, although mostly known as poetry, will help us walk in wisdom. The book of Proverbs contains some of the most useful bits of guidance and instruction in the Scriptures. One of the most quoted texts in Proverbs is right at the beginning: "The fear of the LORD is the beginning of knowledge" (Prov. 1:7).

If we desire to gain knowledge and wisdom, we'll need to start with the fear of the Lord. As I wrote in Week 9, we don't want to pursue knowledge simply to know more in order to boast about how much we know or to feel good about ourselves. Knowing God is more than knowing *about* God. Our natural inclination is to start with reading and studying. But as we'll see later in our plan, knowledge tends to puff up (1 Cor. 8:1). But when coupled with reverence and awe, our knowledge leads to worship and obedience.

Knowledge without the fear of the Lord could lead to pride or even abuse. Knowledge could never be truly wise without fearing the Lord. So, as we read and study God's Word, let's pray that it leads to worship. We need a greater reverence of Him so we might truly gain wisdom and knowledge.

IDEAS FOR YOUR REST DAY

Catch up on any missed reading.

Pause to study a text or chapter using your favorite Bible study method.

Identify a person or situation in the text, and learn more about their story.

Proverbs 9

to

Proverbs 31

1 What do you learn about God and His character in these verses?

2 Where is Jesus in these chapters? Where do you see the gospel?

3 How might you apply these verses to your life?

DAY 1 • *Read* Proverbs 9–12

DAY 2 • *Read* Proverbs 13–16

Say or write your prayer:

1 What do you learn about God and His character in these verses?
2 Where is Jesus in these chapters? Where do you see the gospel?
3 How might you apply these verses to your life?

DAY 3 • *Read* Proverbs 17–20

DAY 4 • *Read* Proverbs 21–23

Say or write your prayer:

1 What do you learn about God and His character in these verses?
2 Where is Jesus in these chapters? Where do you see the gospel?
3 How might you apply these verses to your life?

DAY 5 • *Read* Proverbs 24–27

DAY 6 • *Read* Proverbs 28–31

Say or write your prayer:

Save Yourself Grief

Retribution and revenge are the knee-jerk responses to a conflict, but most of us won't end up in court (Prov. 25:8). What's likely our temptation is to share our grievances with others. However, if we look closely at these verses, the warning isn't focused on how our gossip affects the other person (vv. 9, 10). The focus is on how gossip affects the one who shares about the grievance. You never want to take a text out of context, nor do you want to misapply it. For example, this text should not be used to conceal sexual abuse.

Considering all of the caveats, there are other texts in the Scriptures that give clear and helpful instructions for conflict resolution (the well-known verses in Matthew 18:15–22 and Luke 12:57–59 about a brother or sister sinning against us, for example). If the conflict can be kept between two parties, we can strive to do that. But that isn't our first instinct. Often our instinct is to talk about a grievance with those not involved and share in a way that puffs us up and states our case alone. But as we see in Proverbs, it can cause more strife and pain and sorrow . . . for us! Instead of our self-sabotaging tendencies, we can ask God for self-control and patience that He will exact justice so we can rest.

**IDEAS
FOR YOUR
REST DAY**

Catch up on any missed reading.

Pause to study a text or chapter using your favorite Bible study method.

Identify a person or situation in the text, and learn more about their story.

Ecclesiastes 1

to

Isaiah 7

Consider

1 What do you learn about God and His character in these verses?
2 Where is Jesus in these chapters? Where do you see the gospel?
3 How might you apply these verses to your life?

DAY 1 • *Read* Ecclesiastes 1–6

DAY 2 • *Read* Ecclesiastes 7–12

Say or write your prayer:

Consider

1 What do you learn about God and His character in these verses?
2 Where is Jesus in these chapters? Where do you see the gospel?
3 How might you apply these verses to your life?

DAY 3 • *Read* Song of Solomon 1–4

DAY 4 • *Read* Song of Solomon 5–8

Say or write your prayer:

Consider

1 What do you learn about God and His character in these verses?
2 Where is Jesus in these chapters? Where do you see the gospel?
3 How might you apply these verses to your life?

DAY 5 • *Read* Isaiah 1–3

DAY 6 • *Read* Isaiah 4–7

Say or write your prayer:

Three Books, One Message

I'm not sure if we've had a week like this yet. We've hit three different books of the Bible, each quite different in message and style. Should I write about the meaninglessness or temporality of earthly pursuits or the sensuality of marriage and how much God loves us, or do I reflect on the coming of the Lord? There is one tie that binds them: Jesus. Jesus is the only person who can and will fully satisfy us. We may pursue other things, whether worldly positions or even the gift of marriage, but none can play the lead role in our hearts.

In a life that may feel meaningless, Jesus is the One who remains constant. Times change, He does not. Through all of life's ups and downs, trials and sorrows, and the seemingly mundane, Jesus remains the One who not only lays down His life for His bride, but also goes and pursues the lost sheep. And Isaiah has already ushered us through the awesome throne room of a holy God to the prophecy of Immanuel, God with us. So, as we reflect on the prophecy of our Lord and Savior throughout Isaiah, we also proclaim Maranatha—come, our Lord. We long for you. We desire you.

IDEAS
FOR YOUR
REST DAY

Catch up on any missed reading.

Pause to study a text or chapter using your favorite Bible study method.

Identify a person or situation in the text, and learn more about their story.

Isaiah 8
to
Isaiah 31

1 What do you learn about God and His character in these verses?
2 Where is Jesus in these chapters? Where do you see the gospel?
3 How might you apply these verses to your life?

DAY 1 • *Read* Isaiah 8–10

DAY 2 • *Read* Isaiah 11–14

Say or write your prayer:

Consider

1 What do you learn about God and His character in these verses?
2 Where is Jesus in these chapters? Where do you see the gospel?
3 How might you apply these verses to your life?

DAY 3 • _Read_ Isaiah 15–19

DAY 4 • _Read_ Isaiah 20–24

Say or write your prayer:

Consider

1 What do you learn about God and His character in these verses?
2 Where is Jesus in these chapters? Where do you see the gospel?
3 How might you apply these verses to your life?

DAY 5 • *Read* Isaiah 25–28

DAY 6 • *Read* Isaiah 29–31

Say or write your prayer:

Christmas All Year Long

If I asked you what verse was most referenced every year at Christmastime, I imagine most of you would recite Isaiah 9:6:

> For to us a child is born,
>   to us a son is given;
> and the government shall be upon his shoulder,
>   and his name shall be called
> Wonderful Counselor, Mighty God,
>   Everlasting Father, Prince of Peace.

Isaiah prophesied of a baby who will save the world. This was a surprising and amazing announcement because it was coming to a rebellious people. But there were also wars and unrest. There was no peace to be found.

But then we see Isaiah speak of a victory of sorts. There will be a glorious life, joy, and victory for God's people. We see that in verses 1 through 5. But how? A child. A son is given. We see it repeated in the gospel of Luke: "For unto you is born this day in the city of David a Savior, who is Christ the Lord" (Luke 2:11).

When there's unrest and confusion in our nation, we can rest knowing that we have a just, eternal King. When we need wisdom, we can call upon our Wonderful Counselor. When we are weak, we can draw strength from our mighty God. We can rejoice knowing that because of Him we will never be separated from our everlasting Father. And when everything around is chaotic, we lean on the Prince of Peace.

Aren't we glad that our Immanuel is here!

IDEAS FOR YOUR REST DAY

Catch up on any missed reading.

Pause to study a text or chapter using your favorite Bible study method.

Identify a person or situation in the text, and learn more about their story.

Isaiah 32
to
Isaiah 50

Consider	1 What do you learn about God and His character in these verses?
	2 Where is Jesus in these chapters? Where do you see the gospel?
	3 How might you apply these verses to your life?

DAY 1 • *Read* Isaiah 32–35

DAY 2 • *Read* Isaiah 36–38

Say or write your prayer:

1 What do you learn about God and His character in these verses?

2 Where is Jesus in these chapters? Where do you see the gospel?

3 How might you apply these verses to your life?

DAY 3 • *Read* Isaiah 39–41

DAY 4 • *Read* Isaiah 42–44

Say or write your prayer:

1 What do you learn about God and His character in these verses?
2 Where is Jesus in these chapters? Where do you see the gospel?
3 How might you apply these verses to your life?

DAY 5 • *Read* Isaiah 45–47

DAY 6 • *Read* Isaiah 48–50

Say or write your prayer:

No Justice, No Peace

Isaiah 42 is a song and prophecy about Jesus, God's chosen servant. The first few verses address His character. I tend to pause and reflect on the gentleness of the Lord. But as my eyes continue to be opened to the injustice of the world I need the reminder in verse 4: God is a just God. When we think of justice, we often think of vengeance and punishment. Evil will be extinguished by God's wrath. But have you ever considered that God's justice brings peace?

Justice isn't only about wrath or payment for wrongdoing, it's about making things right, making things new. Expounding on this verse, the *Moody Bible Commentary* puts it like this:

> Bringing justice will also bring peace as even the nations (the coastlands) will wait to hear the Servant's instruction. The Servant will persevere until He completes His mission. He will establish justice on the earth and the nations will no longer set their own rules. Instead, they will align themselves with the law of the Servant.[1]

I don't pretend to understand how it will all happen, but it does bring me peace to imagine a world that submits to King Jesus and a gentle, lowly, and just God.

**IDEAS
FOR YOUR
REST DAY**

Catch up on any missed reading.

Pause to study a text or chapter using your favorite Bible study method.

Identify a person or situation in the text, and learn more about their story.

Isaiah 51
to
Jeremiah 3

1 What do you learn about God and His character in these verses?
2 Where is Jesus in these chapters? Where do you see the gospel?
3 How might you apply these verses to your life?

DAY 1 • *Read* Isaiah 51–53

DAY 2 • *Read* Isaiah 54–57

Say or write your prayer:

Consider | 1 What do you learn about God and His character in these verses?
2 Where is Jesus in these chapters? Where do you see the gospel?
3 How might you apply these verses to your life?

DAY 3 • *Read* Isaiah 58–60

DAY 4 • *Read* Isaiah 61–64

Say or write your prayer:

Consider	1 What do you learn about God and His character in these verses?
	2 Where is Jesus in these chapters? Where do you see the gospel?
	3 How might you apply these verses to your life?

DAY 5 • *Read* Isaiah 65–66

_____

_____

_____

_____

_____

DAY 6 • *Read* Jeremiah 1–3

_____

_____

_____

_____

_____

Say or write your prayer:

A Prophecy Worth Believing

I saiah 53 provides a detailed and grim description of how Jesus would be received and what He would endure. The contrast of what we did versus what He did for us is humbling. Frankly, it takes faith to believe.

He was wounded for our transgressions and crushed for our iniquities. He endured it all because of us, *for* us. If this is true, why would we ever not trust Him to forgive our every sin? His utterly brutal death provides our peace with God and heals us from sin. We might believe this intellectually, but do we live and walk in this knowledge? If we walk in guilt and condemnation for repented-of and forgiven sin, then we are not believing that what we read in Isaiah 53 is true, at least not for us.

If it *is* true, then you and I can rest from trying to earn our salvation. Legalism is an assault on grace. If we believe what we've read, then we must believe that His death was enough. We can never do enough or be enough. God must do the work of salvation—once and for all. Jesus paid it all. So maybe the question isn't, "Is this true?" but rather, "Do you believe?" Let's ask the Lord to help us believe that Jesus fulfilled Isaiah's prophecy and rest in God's unearned favor.

IDEAS FOR YOUR REST DAY

Catch up on any missed reading.

Pause to study a text or chapter using your favorite Bible study method.

Identify a person or situation in the text, and learn more about their story.

Jeremiah 4

to

Jeremiah 21

1 What do you learn about God and His character in these verses?
2 Where is Jesus in these chapters? Where do you see the gospel?
3 How might you apply these verses to your life?

DAY 1 • *Read* Jeremiah 4–5

DAY 2 • *Read* Jeremiah 6–8

Say or write your prayer:

1 What do you learn about God and His character in these verses?
2 Where is Jesus in these chapters? Where do you see the gospel?
3 How might you apply these verses to your life?

DAY 3 · *Read* Jeremiah 9–11

DAY 4 · *Read* Jeremiah 12–14

Say or write your prayer:

Consider

1 What do you learn about God and His character in these verses?
2 Where is Jesus in these chapters? Where do you see the gospel?
3 How might you apply these verses to your life?

DAY 5 • *Read* Jeremiah 15–17

DAY 6 • *Read* Jeremiah 18–21

Say or write your prayer:

Is Your Heart Desperately Sick?

At the beginning of Jeremiah 17, the prophet addresses Judah's idolatry and apparent worship of other men. They are not putting their trust in God. Jeremiah explains that those who trust in God are blessed. Why would a nation choose to trust man over God? Jeremiah gives the answer in verse 9: because the heart is deceitful.

Since Genesis 3, the scenario of a people putting their trust in other human beings rather than God is familiar. We can see this scene being played out over the centuries. And if we are honest with ourselves, we too have at times placed our trust in man over God. But is our heart deceitful above all things and desperately sick? No, not for those who have trusted in the Lord as our Savior.

We have been given a new heart; we are new creations. We have the power to resist temptation. More than that, God does not relate to us as ones whose hearts are deceitful. So, when we read this verse, we don't say, "Aren't we glad we aren't like them?" We *are* like them. Instead, we say, "Aren't we glad that Jesus stands in the gap and covers us with His righteousness?"

IDEAS
FOR YOUR
REST DAY

Catch up on any missed reading.

Pause to study a text or chapter using your favorite Bible study method.

Identify a person or situation in the text, and learn more about their story.

Jeremiah 22
to
Jeremiah 38

Consider

1 What do you learn about God and His character in these verses?
2 Where is Jesus in these chapters? Where do you see the gospel?
3 How might you apply these verses to your life?

DAY 1 • *Read* Jeremiah 22–24

DAY 2 • *Read* Jeremiah 25–27

Say or write your prayer:

1 What do you learn about God and His character in these verses?
2 Where is Jesus in these chapters? Where do you see the gospel?
3 How might you apply these verses to your life?

DAY 3 • *Read* Jeremiah 28–30

DAY 4 • *Read* Jeremiah 31–32

Say or write your prayer:

1 What do you learn about God and His character in these verses?
2 Where is Jesus in these chapters? Where do you see the gospel?
3 How might you apply these verses to your life?

DAY 5 • *Read* Jeremiah 33–35

DAY 6 • *Read* Jeremiah 36–38

Say or write your prayer:

Redeeming Jeremiah 29:11

Jeremiah 29:11 is likely one of the most misused and misinterpreted Scriptures in all of the Bible. It's a wonderful promise. It's also a promise to the exiles in Babylon. When God promises to prosper the exiles, many today interpret it as God promising financial gain to the Christian. This misapplication and misinterpretation of the text is not only false but dreadfully harmful. God never promised His people wealth.

Although we should be cautious trying to directly apply this verse to our lives, and we never want to take something out of context and misinterpret it, God's words to those in exile do hold lessons for us today. One that stands out is God's sovereignty over their lives. The same God who planned their days is the same God who plans our days. We can rest and have peace knowing that we are in the hands of a good and sovereign God.

IDEAS FOR YOUR REST DAY

Catch up on any missed reading.

Pause to study a text or chapter using your favorite Bible study method.

Identify a person or situation in the text, and learn more about their story.

Jeremiah 39

to

Lamentations 2

1 What do you learn about God and His character in these verses?

2 Where is Jesus in these chapters? Where do you see the gospel?

3 How might you apply these verses to your life?

DAY 1 • *Read* Jeremiah 39–42

DAY 2 • *Read* Jeremiah 43–46

Say or write your prayer:

Consider

1 What do you learn about God and His character in these verses?
2 Where is Jesus in these chapters? Where do you see the gospel?
3 How might you apply these verses to your life?

DAY 3 • *Read* Jeremiah 47–48

DAY 4 • *Read* Jeremiah 49–50

Say or write your prayer:

Consider

1 What do you learn about God and His character in these verses?
2 Where is Jesus in these chapters? Where do you see the gospel?
3 How might you apply these verses to your life?

DAY 5 • *Read* Jeremiah 51–52

DAY 6 • *Read* Lamentations 1–2

Say or write your prayer:

Let's Study Jeremiah 31 and the New Covenant

To break up the density of our reading this week, let's pause and study Jeremiah 31. If you need to catch up on your reading, feel free to skip this reflection and keep reading instead. Grab a piece of paper or write in the space provided on your Rest Day.

Turn to Jeremiah 31. Using a basic Bible study method, you are going to:

1. Read the chapter.

2. Observe: ask questions like who, what, when, where, why, and how. Write out your answers.

3. Interpret: What does the text mean? What's the context? How does it relate to the rest of Scripture? Write out your answers.

4. Apply: Is there context for me today? Write out your answer, and pray for the Lord's help to apply what you have learned.

5. I always make sure to ask: What does the text say about the character of God and/or how does it point to Jesus? Write out your answer.

There's such hope here of God's never-ending commitment to Israel. Take a peek at Luke 22:19–20. Jesus makes the same commitment to all of humanity. God truly is a covenant-keeping God.

I hope that you enjoyed this brief break to study. Feel free to use this method anytime you'd like to dig a little deeper during your reading time.

IDEAS FOR YOUR REST DAY	
	Catch up on any missed reading.
	Pause to study a text or chapter using your favorite Bible study method.
	Identify a person or situation in the text, and learn more about their story.

Lamentations 3
to
Ezekiel 19

	1 What do you learn about God and His character in these verses?
Consider	2 Where is Jesus in these chapters? Where do you see the gospel?
	3 How might you apply these verses to your life?

DAY 1 • *Read* Lamentations 3–5

DAY 2 • *Read* Ezekiel 1–4

Say or write your prayer:

1 What do you learn about God and His character in these verses?

2 Where is Jesus in these chapters? Where do you see the gospel?

3 How might you apply these verses to your life?

DAY 3 • *Read* Ezekiel 5–9

DAY 4 • *Read* Ezekiel 10–13

Say or write your prayer:

1 What do you learn about God and His character in these verses?
2 Where is Jesus in these chapters? Where do you see the gospel?
3 How might you apply these verses to your life?

DAY 5 • *Read* Ezekiel 14–16

DAY 6 • *Read* Ezekiel 17–19

Say or write your prayer:

New Every Morning

Although we are deep into Ezekiel, I wanted to look back at the beginning of the week and a cherished text in Lamentations 3:22–24. I believe these are the most hopeful words in Lamentations. In the midst of intense suffering and sorrow, a reminder that the steadfast love of the Lord never ceases is comforting. They remind me of the lyrics in the hymn, "On Christ the Solid Rock I Stand": "When all around my soul gives way, he then is all my hope and stay."[1]

I remember a season of long-suffering when almost every morning I'd pray for the Lord to give me new mercies to get through that day. I knew that I wouldn't have instant relief, but I trusted that if I called on the Lord, He would hear me. So I cried out. He was faithful to give me what I needed for that day—every morning, new mercies.

These words became a lifeline:

> The steadfast love of the LORD never ceases;
>   his mercies never come to an end;
> they are new every morning;
>   great is your faithfulness.
> "The LORD is my portion," says my soul,
>   "therefore I will hope in him." (Lam. 3:22–24)

His mercies never come to an end, but in our deep distress, it can be difficult to remember God is always merciful. He is always faithful. There is a never-ending reminder of His grace—it's new every morning. Every sunrise, we can remember God is near and faithful.

IDEAS FOR YOUR REST DAY

Catch up on any missed reading.

Pause to study a text or chapter using your favorite Bible study method.

Identify a person or situation in the text, and learn more about their story.

In the seventh year, in th

on the tenth day of the r

of the elders of Israel ca

the LORD, and sat befor

word of the LORD cam

man, speak to the elders

say to them, Thus says th

Is it to inquire of me tha

I live, declares the Lord

be inquired of by you. W

them, son of man, will y

Let them know the abor

their fathers, and say to

says the Lord GOD: On

I chose Israel, I swore to

WEEK 36

Ezekiel 20
to
Ezekiel 36

1 What do you learn about God and His character in these verses?
2 Where is Jesus in these chapters? Where do you see the gospel?
3 How might you apply these verses to your life?

DAY 1 • *Read* Ezekiel 20–21

DAY 2 • *Read* Ezekiel 22–24

Say or write your prayer:

1 What do you learn about God and His character in these verses?
2 Where is Jesus in these chapters? Where do you see the gospel?
3 How might you apply these verses to your life?

DAY 3 • *Read* Ezekiel 25–27

DAY 4 • *Read* Ezekiel 28–30

Say or write your prayer:

Consider

1 What do you learn about God and His character in these verses?
2 Where is Jesus in these chapters? Where do you see the gospel?
3 How might you apply these verses to your life?

DAY 5 • *Read* Ezekiel 31–33

DAY 6 • *Read* Ezekiel 34–36

Say or write your prayer:

Life to Our Dry Bones

E zekiel 37:3–5 tells an amazing story of the prophet's vision:

> He said to me, "Son of man, can these bones live?" And I
> answered, "O Lord GOD, you know." Then he said to me,
> "Prophesy over these bones, and say to them, O dry bones, hear
> the word of the LORD. Thus says the Lord GOD to these bones:
> Behold, I will cause breath to enter you, and you shall live."

You have not come to chapter 37 in Ezekiel yet. So far in Ezekiel, we have read about destruction, idolatry, and utter hopelessness. Babylon had destroyed the Jewish people, and all seemed lost. Can Ezekiel prophesy hope in dismal circumstances? Is *anything* impossible for the Lord? Consider these verses above a preview of hope. In your next reading, you will encounter a future for them and for you and me.

God breathes life into dry, dead bones. A life that is both spiritual (new life) and physical (resurrection). Jesus defeated sin and death and one day we will experience the ultimate defeat of death forever. In the midst of sin and rebellion, captivity and hopelessness, God reminded His people that He would not abandon them. Even in His judgment, He was promising them eternal hope.

As author Chris Bruno writes:

> So the promise of Ezekiel 37 was that once sin was defeated,
> the power of death would be removed. And once the power of
> death was removed, God's Spirit would have free rein to give
> life—first to the servant, and then to all those who receive the
> forgiveness of sin promised in the new covenant and won by
> the servant's death. Through this vision in Ezekiel 37, God was
> promising a new creation![1]

God never deserts His people, and because of Jesus, we are counted among them! We who have the New Testament can have even greater confidence and hope in the imagery of new life. God breathes life into our mortal bodies and will one day defeat death forevermore.

Catch up on any missed reading.

Pause to study a text or chapter using your favorite Bible study method.

Identify a person or situation in the text, and learn more about their story.

Ezekiel 37
to
Daniel 6

Consider

1 What do you learn about God and His character in these verses?
2 Where is Jesus in these chapters? Where do you see the gospel?
3 How might you apply these verses to your life?

DAY 1 • *Read* Ezekiel 37–39

DAY 2 • *Read* Ezekiel 40–42

Say or write your prayer:

Consider

1 What do you learn about God and His character in these verses?
2 Where is Jesus in these chapters? Where do you see the gospel?
3 How might you apply these verses to your life?

DAY 3 • *Read* Ezekiel 43–45

DAY 4 • *Read* Ezekiel 46–48

Say or write your prayer:

1 What do you learn about God and His character in these verses?
2 Where is Jesus in these chapters? Where do you see the gospel?
3 How might you apply these verses to your life?

DAY 5 • *Read* Daniel 1–3

DAY 6 • *Read* Daniel 4–6

Say or write your prayer:

Faith That Leads to Prayer

Pause and reread Daniel 6:10–28.

Lord willing, we'll never find ourselves opposed by leaders, entrenched in a conspiracy to overthrow us, and sentenced to death by lions! But I do pray that in whatever situation we are in, we have the faith of Daniel (Heb. 11:32–34). His faith led him to pray in the midst of dire circumstances (Dan. 6:10).

Hebrews 11:33 reminds us that in the face of a lion, Daniel had faith and believed God could save him. Daniel didn't pray because he knew what God was going to do. He had no idea. He prayed because he knew the God who could do it. No matter the circumstance, we can turn to God in prayer. As R. C. Sproul wrote in his book *Knowing Scripture*: "The issue of faith is not so much whether we believe in God, but whether we believe the God we believe in."[1]

IDEAS
FOR YOUR
REST DAY

Catch up on any missed reading.

Pause to study a text or chapter using your favorite Bible study method.

Identify a person or situation in the text, and learn more about their story.

Daniel 7
to
Joel 3

1 What do you learn about God and His character in these verses?
2 Where is Jesus in these chapters? Where do you see the gospel?
3 How might you apply these verses to your life?

DAY 1 • *Read* Daniel 7–9

DAY 2 • *Read* Daniel 10–12

Say or write your prayer:

1 What do you learn about God and His character in these verses?
2 Where is Jesus in these chapters? Where do you see the gospel?
3 How might you apply these verses to your life?

DAY 3 • *Read* Hosea 1–4

DAY 4 • *Read* Hosea 5–9

Say or write your prayer:

1 What do you learn about God and His character in these verses?
2 Where is Jesus in these chapters? Where do you see the gospel?
3 How might you apply these verses to your life?

DAY 5 • *Read* Hosea 10–14

DAY 6 • *Read* Joel 1–3

Say or write your prayer:

God Wants Our Heart

Joel is a short prophetic book about God's judgment over Israel and all the nations (Joel 3:2–3). But within this short book is a hopeful call to repentance. A major theme and refrain in the book of Joel is "the day of the Lord," referring to the day that the Lord will bring His final judgment. But it isn't a message of doom. Joel tells the people that if they repent, the Lord will spare them. Joel 2:12–13 is not only a theme of repentance in the book, but one we see throughout the Bible:

> "Yet even now," declares the LORD,
> "return to me with all your heart,
> with fasting, with weeping, and with mourning;
> and rend your hearts and not your garments."
> Return to the LORD your God,
> for he is gracious and merciful,
> slow to anger, and abounding in steadfast love;
> and he relents over disaster.

God is after our hearts; He is not interested in our religious rituals. He wants us to repent—turn to Him. He will not turn us away. Instead, the Lord is gracious and merciful, slow to anger, and abounding in love. This is our God! Haven't we heard this before? Won't we read it again? Yes!

Although we may not experience the same plagues and destruction as the ones in this story, I can't help but think maybe the Lord is also warning us. Repentance leads to freedom; sin leads to death. We can, by God's grace, choose to walk in freedom and receive His mercy and love.

**IDEAS
FOR YOUR
REST DAY**

Catch up on any missed reading.

Pause to study a text or chapter using your favorite Bible study method.

Identify a person or situation in the text, and learn more about their story.

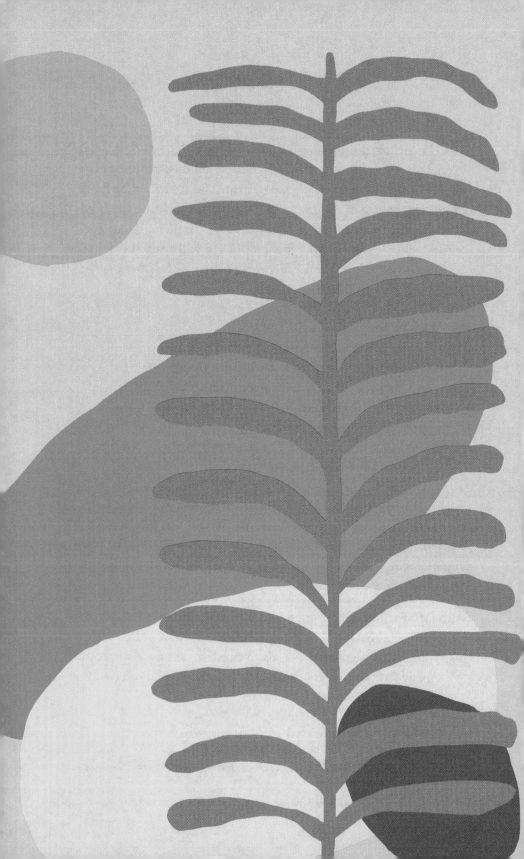

·

WEEK 39

·

Amos 1
to
Micah 7

1 What do you learn about God and His character in these verses?
2 Where is Jesus in these chapters? Where do you see the gospel?
3 How might you apply these verses to your life?

DAY 1 • *Read* Amos 1–4

DAY 2 • *Read* Amos 5–9

Say or write your prayer:

Consider	1	What do you learn about God and His character in these verses?
	2	Where is Jesus in these chapters? Where do you see the gospel?
	3	How might you apply these verses to your life?

DAY 3 • *Read* Obadiah

***

DAY 4 • *Read* Jonah 1–4

***

Say or write your prayer:

1 What do you learn about God and His character in these verses?
2 Where is Jesus in these chapters? Where do you see the gospel?
3 How might you apply these verses to your life?

DAY 5 • *Read* Micah 1–4

DAY 6 • *Read* Micah 5–7

Say or write your prayer:

A Short Book
Packed with History

O badiah is a short book. In fact, it's the shortest in the Old Testament. But within his short prophetic book is a brief history lesson on Jacob, Esau, and the continued hostility between these two ancestral lines. If you noticed, the Lord began to call Edom "Esau" (v. 6), and Israel "Jacob" (v. 10). To more fully understand, we need to go back to Genesis 25:23 and 27:39–40. Through the treatment of Edom toward Judah, we see that the descendants of Jacob and Esau were fulfilling the relationship that was foreshadowed in Genesis.

As I noted in my reflection in our first week, if we can grasp what is happening in the book of Genesis, we will understand the entire Bible. As we read Obadiah, that statement stands true. We find glimpses of Obadiah not only in Genesis but also in other places in the Old Testament, so I encourage you to study it (see Lamentations or Jeremiah 49). Obadiah prophesied God's judgment over Edom because of the people's violence and apathy toward Israel (vv. 10–14).[1] But God's judgment isn't the final word. At the end of the book— just as God had always promised—we see that God will restore His kingdom and the land will experience redemption. And as a friend said to me recently, God's judgment is our assurance of God's justice.

IDEAS
FOR YOUR
REST DAY

Catch up on any missed reading.

Pause to study a text or chapter using your favorite Bible study method.

Identify a person or situation in the text, and learn more about their story.

Nahum 1

to

Zechariah 10

1 What do you learn about God and His character in these verses?
2 Where is Jesus in these chapters? Where do you see the gospel?
3 How might you apply these verses to your life?

DAY 1 • *Read* Nahum 1–3

DAY 2 • *Read* Habakkuk 1–3

Say or write your prayer:

1 What do you learn about God and His character in these verses?
2 Where is Jesus in these chapters? Where do you see the gospel?
3 How might you apply these verses to your life?

DAY 3 • *Read* Zephaniah 1–3

DAY 4 • *Read* Haggai 1–2

Say or write your prayer:

1 What do you learn about God and His character in these verses?
2 Where is Jesus in these chapters? Where do you see the gospel?
3 How might you apply these verses to your life?

DAY 5 • *Read* Zechariah 1–6

DAY 6 • *Read* Zechariah 7–10

Say or write your prayer:

Yet I Will Rejoice

The prophet Habakkuk questioned God's action and lack of justice for Judah. Although the book is classified as a prophetic book, it reads a lot like a lament. However, at the end of this short book are rich verses that we can all relate to and apply. Habakkuk has turned his frustrations and confusion to praise and faith.

> Though the fig tree should not blossom,
>   nor fruit be on the vines,
> the produce of the olive fail
>   and the fields yield no food,
> the flock be cut off from the fold
>   and there be no herd in the stalls,
> yet I will rejoice in the LORD;
>   I will take joy in the God of my salvation.
> GOD, the Lord, is my strength;
>   he makes my feet like the deer's;
>   he makes me tread on my high places.
> (Hab. 3:17–19)

We may not ever experience the anxiety of seeing a nation invading and destroying our land and people, but we will likely feel barren, dry, and empty at some point in our walk with the Lord. We will experience a trial that might lead us to ask, "Where is God in this?" We can pray that at the end of our lament, like Habakkuk and many saints before and after him, we will be able to say, "Yet I will rejoice in the Lord." Our sustaining joy comes not in our circumstances; it comes in the God of our salvation.

IDEAS
FOR YOUR
REST DAY

Catch up on any missed reading.

Pause to study a text or chapter using your favorite Bible study method.

Identify a person or situation in the text, and learn more about their story.

Zechariah 11
to
Matthew 15

Consider

1 What do you learn about God and His character in these verses?
2 Where is Jesus in these chapters? Where do you see the gospel?
3 How might you apply these verses to your life?

DAY 1 • *Read* Zechariah 11–14

DAY 2 • *Read* Malachi 1–4

Say or write your prayer:

1 What do you learn about God and His character in these verses?

2 Where is Jesus in these chapters? Where do you see the gospel?

3 How might you apply these verses to your life?

DAY 3 • *Read* Matthew 1–5

DAY 4 • *Read* Matthew 6–9

Say or write your prayer:

1 What do you learn about God and His character in these verses?
2 Where is Jesus in these chapters? Where do you see the gospel?
3 How might you apply these verses to your life?

DAY 5 • *Read* Matthew 10–12

DAY 6 • *Read* Matthew 13–15

Say or write your prayer:

Entering the New, Remembering the Old

This week, for the first time, we have entered the New Testament. As I read through Matthew, I couldn't help but think about all the Old Testament saints who died waiting and longing for the coming Savior. Each died trusting in the promise. Here we are watching as prophecies are fulfilled and promises are kept. Yet Matthew starts with a genealogy, taking us right back to the beginning of time.

Spending time in the Old Testament is important in order to fully grasp what is happening in the New. People like Abraham, Isaac, Tamar, Salmon, Rahab, Boaz, Ruth, Jesse, and King David take us down our Bible reading plan memory lane. Even God's genealogy proves His words that all of Scripture points back to Him:

"You search the Scriptures because you think that in them you have eternal life; and it is they that bear witness about me" (John 5:39).

IDEAS FOR YOUR REST DAY

Catch up on any missed reading.

Pause to study a text or chapter using your favorite Bible study method.

Identify a person or situation in the text, and learn more about their story.

WEEK 42

Matthew 16

to

Mark 7

1 What do you learn about God and His character in these verses?
2 Where is Jesus in these chapters? Where do you see the gospel?
3 How might you apply these verses to your life?

DAY 1 • *Read* Matthew 16–20

DAY 2 • *Read* Matthew 21–23

Say or write your prayer:

Consider

1 What do you learn about God and His character in these verses?
2 Where is Jesus in these chapters? Where do you see the gospel?
3 How might you apply these verses to your life?

DAY 3 • *Read* Matthew 24–25

DAY 4 • *Read* Matthew 26–28

Say or write your prayer:

1 What do you learn about God and His character in these verses?
2 Where is Jesus in these chapters? Where do you see the gospel?
3 How might you apply these verses to your life?

DAY 5 • *Read* Mark 1–4

DAY 6 • *Read* Mark 5–7

Say or write your prayer:

Follow Me and Make Disciples

I f you've been reading straight through the Bible and have just completed Week 42, you may need a reminder for why we are continuing to read. As much as we hope to gain knowledge, ultimately our goal is to enjoy Jesus. My hope is that like Simon and Andrew, you and I would be eager to drop everything and follow Jesus (Mark 1:17). But Jesus' desire for His disciples wasn't only for them to submit their lives to Him; He wanted to make them fishers of men.

The knowledge we gain about our Savior isn't meant to be stored for ourselves. Yes, we should enjoy the Lord, but what if we take all that we learn and share it with others? Jesus gave His disciples—and by extension us—the command to go and make disciples of all nations, teaching them to obey all that He commanded (Matt. 28:19–20).

Can you believe that we have read almost all that He has commanded? Let's find ways to give it away to those around us.

IDEAS FOR YOUR REST DAY

Catch up on any missed reading.

Pause to study a text or chapter using your favorite Bible study method.

Identify a person or situation in the text, and learn more about their story.

Mark 8

to

Luke 7

1 What do you learn about God and His character in these verses?
2 Where is Jesus in these chapters? Where do you see the gospel?
3 How might you apply these verses to your life?

DAY 1 • *Read* Mark 8–10

DAY 2 • *Read* Mark 11–13

Say or write your prayer:

Consider

1 What do you learn about God and His character in these verses?
2 Where is Jesus in these chapters? Where do you see the gospel?
3 How might you apply these verses to your life?

DAY 3 • *Read* Mark 14–16

DAY 4 • *Read* Luke 1–2

Say or write your prayer:

Consider   1 What do you learn about God and His character in these verses?
2 Where is Jesus in these chapters? Where do you see the gospel?
3 How might you apply these verses to your life?

DAY 5 • *Read* Luke 3–5

_____

_____

_____

_____

_____

DAY 6 • *Read* Luke 6–7

_____

_____

_____

_____

_____

Say or write your prayer:

He Understands

Take a moment to reread Mark 14:32–42.

One of the first times I truly understood Jesus' empathy toward us was when I better understood His experience of praying in the garden of Gethsemane. I can't imagine the agony of knowing all things. We don't know when tragedy will strike, but Jesus was fully aware of every pain He was about to endure—rejection, shame, slander, mocking, beating, and death by crucifixion. He knew it all. He took it all.

And so, when we eventually get to Hebrews 4, we will look back at Jesus in the garden and have a greater appreciation for what it means that Jesus was tempted in every way but without sin (Heb. 4:15). He wasn't only tempted in the wilderness; Jesus was tempted to give up and turn away from His calling. Temptation is never sin, and He understands every temptation and sorrow and pain and suffering that we endure or will endure. When we run to Jesus in our pain, He understands—fully—and He welcomes us.

IDEAS FOR YOUR REST DAY

Catch up on any missed reading.

Pause to study a text or chapter using your favorite Bible study method.

Identify a person or situation in the text, and learn more about their story.

Soon afterward he went
cities and villages, procla
bringing the good news
of God. And the twelve
and also some women w
healed of evil spirits and
Mary, called Magdalene
seven demons had gone
Joanna, the wife of Chuz
household manager, and
many others, who provid
out of their means. And
crowd was gathering and
town after town came to
a parable, "A sower went

Luke 8
to
Luke 24

1 What do you learn about God and His character in these verses?

2 Where is Jesus in these chapters? Where do you see the gospel?

3 How might you apply these verses to your life?

DAY 1 • *Read* Luke 8–9

DAY 2 • *Read* Luke 10–12

Say or write your prayer:

1 What do you learn about God and His character in these verses?
2 Where is Jesus in these chapters? Where do you see the gospel?
3 How might you apply these verses to your life?

DAY 3 • *Read* Luke 13–16

DAY 4 • *Read* Luke 17–19

Say or write your prayer:

1 What do you learn about God and His character in these verses?
2 Where is Jesus in these chapters? Where do you see the gospel?
3 How might you apply these verses to your life?

DAY 5 • *Read* Luke 20–22

DAY 6 • *Read* Luke 23–24

Say or write your prayer:

Jesus and Women

Jesus was accompanied by both men and women as He proclaimed the good news. The brief account in Luke 8:1–3 of the women providing for Jesus and His disciples should be an encouragement to the church. We are all needed for the mission, whether through teaching or support. Jesus not only acknowledged women, He utilized them.

I've always been encouraged by Jesus' interactions with women. He wasn't afraid to associate with them, they show up in His genealogy, He interacted with them alone, He interacted with women from different cultures, and He had female friends that He cared for deeply. And here we see that He allowed them to be a part of His ministry. It's amazing how two sentences in the Bible can inspire and encourage all while mobilizing us to act and be involved in the mission today. God didn't inspire Luke to capture this scene for the world to see for no good reason. He is intentional.

I can't pretend to know God's motives, but considering all of Scripture, I know that He wants all of His people to be involved in His mission. It's His invitation to us. Go and do.

IDEAS
FOR YOUR
REST DAY

Catch up on any missed reading.

Pause to study a text or chapter using your favorite Bible study method.

Identify a person or situation in the text, and learn more about their story.

John 1

to

John 19

	1 What do you learn about God and His character in these verses?
Consider	2 Where is Jesus in these chapters? Where do you see the gospel?
	3 How might you apply these verses to your life?

DAY 1 • *Read* John 1–3

DAY 2 • *Read* John 4–6

Say or write your prayer:

Consider

1 What do you learn about God and His character in these verses?
2 Where is Jesus in these chapters? Where do you see the gospel?
3 How might you apply these verses to your life?

DAY 3 • *Read* John 7–9

DAY 4 • *Read* John 10–12

Say or write your prayer:

1 What do you learn about God and His character in these verses?
2 Where is Jesus in these chapters? Where do you see the gospel?
3 How might you apply these verses to your life?

DAY 5 • *Read* John 13–16

DAY 6 • *Read* John 17–19

Say or write your prayer:

He's in the Beginning

When I'm studying the Bible, I'll often spend months poring over one verse or chapter of the Bible. Almost every verse is packed with meaning . . . and could take a lifetime to unpack. For example, we could meditate on John 1:1–5 for months—for the rest of our lives. "In the beginning was the Word" and the verses that follow make for the most unique, and theologically rich, introduction of any of the Gospels.

John illuminates the existence of Jesus since the beginning of time. He confirms His deity. The text helps us understand that Jesus created all things. Not only did Jesus create the light that fills the night sky and the morning sun, He is the light of the world (a theme you'll see in all of John's writings). His pure light shines in this world that has been darkened by the Fall. The darkness can never overcome the light of our Savior. These verses pack so much truth in so few words.

IDEAS
FOR YOUR
REST DAY

Catch up on any missed reading.

Pause to study a text or chapter using your favorite Bible study method.

Identify a person or situation in the text, and learn more about their story.

WEEK 46

John 20
to
Acts 18

1 What do you learn about God and His character in these verses?
2 Where is Jesus in these chapters? Where do you see the gospel?
3 How might you apply these verses to your life?

DAY 1 • *Read* John 20–21

DAY 2 • *Read* Acts 1–4

Say or write your prayer:

1 What do you learn about God and His character in these verses?

2 Where is Jesus in these chapters? Where do you see the gospel?

3 How might you apply these verses to your life?

DAY 3 • *Read* Acts 5–7

DAY 4 • *Read* Acts 8–10

Say or write your prayer:

Consider	1 What do you learn about God and His character in these verses?
	2 Where is Jesus in these chapters? Where do you see the gospel?
	3 How might you apply these verses to your life?

DAY 5 • *Read* Acts 11–14

DAY 6 • *Read* Acts 15–18

Say or write your prayer:

God, Our Redeemer

The book of Acts reminds me of the book of Genesis. A lot of Bible characters are included, and a lot of events are happening all at once, many significant events. The gospel message is moving with power, but so is the opposition to the gospel. In Acts 7:54–60, we read about the stoning of Stephen. The account of his stoning is significant because it is the first Christian martyrdom recorded in the Bible.

Stephen was preaching the good news and likely healing the sick (Acts 6:8). A certain group of Jews became enraged and instigated the high priests to question Stephen's teaching. Stephen did not retreat, and instead, continued to preach. By the end of his speech, the entire crowd was also enraged and stoned him.

There's a lesson in boldness here but also one of redemption. Standing among the murderers was their leader, Saul (Acts 7:58). Over the next few weeks, the majority of the epistles (letters to followers of Jesus and the early churches) we will enjoy reading were written by Saul, also named Paul. At a scene where we lament the martyrdom of a great saint, we marvel at future grace—the power of the gospel Stephen preached would one day transform the evil Saul into a man who would lead the entire first-century church.

IDEAS FOR YOUR REST DAY	Catch up on any missed reading.
	Pause to study a text or chapter using your favorite Bible study method.
	Identify a person or situation in the text, and learn more about their story.

Acts 19
to
Romans 12

1 What do you learn about God and His character in these verses?
2 Where is Jesus in these chapters? Where do you see the gospel?
3 How might you apply these verses to your life?

DAY 1 • *Read* Acts 19–21

DAY 2 • *Read* Acts 22–25

Say or write your prayer:

| 1 What do you learn about God and His character in these verses?
| 2 Where is Jesus in these chapters? Where do you see the gospel?
| 3 How might you apply these verses to your life?

DAY 3 • *Read* Acts 26–28

DAY 4 • *Read* Romans 1–4

Say or write your prayer:

Consider	1 What do you learn about God and His character in these verses?
	2 Where is Jesus in these chapters? Where do you see the gospel?
	3 How might you apply these verses to your life?

DAY 5 • *Read* Romans 5–8

DAY 6 • *Read* Romans 9–12

Say or write your prayer:

The Road to Salvation

By the time we get to the book of Romans, Paul has been converted to Christianity, and the church is spreading to the ends of the earth. Paul's letter to Rome is one of the most significant epistles in the New Testament. All, of course, are important, but this particular letter is central to understanding the gospel, and the gospel is the theme of the book (Rom. 1:16–17).

With a quick online search, you can find numerous articles on the "Romans Road"—a map through the book of Romans for evangelism.[1] I'm not sure there's a better way to end a week in Romans than to pause and meditate on its theme. Be encouraged as you take your own trip down the Romans Road:

Romans 3:23: "For all have sinned and fall short of the glory of God."

Romans 6:23 teaches us about the consequences of sin: "For the wages of sin is death, but the free gift of God is eternal life through Christ Jesus our Lord."

Romans 10:9: "If you confess with your mouth that Jesus is Lord and believe in your heart that God raised him from the dead, you will be saved."

Romans 10:13: "For 'everyone who calls on the name of the Lord will be saved.'"

Romans 5:1: "Therefore, since we have been justified by faith, we have peace with God through our Lord Jesus Christ."

Romans 8:1: "There is therefore now no condemnation for those who are in Christ Jesus."

Romans 8:38–39: "For I am sure that neither death nor life, nor angels nor rulers, nor things present nor things to come, nor powers, nor height nor depth, nor anything else in all creation, will be able to separate us from the love of God in Christ Jesus our Lord."

The gospel is not only for personal evangelism. It's for the professing Christian too. We all need a reminder of the good things God has done through the life, death, and resurrection of Jesus Christ, our Lord.

Catch up on any missed reading.

Pause to study a text or chapter using your favorite Bible study method.

Identify a person or situation in the text, and learn more about their story.

Let every person be sub
governing authorities. F
no authority except from
those that exist have be
by God. Therefore who
the authorities resists w
appointed, and those w
incur judgment. For rul
terror to good conduct,
Would you have no fea
is in authority? Then do
and you will receive his
he is God's servant for y
if you do wrong, be afra

Romans 13

to

2 Corinthians 7

1 What do you learn about God and His character in these verses?
2 Where is Jesus in these chapters? Where do you see the gospel?
3 How might you apply these verses to your life?

DAY 1 • *Read* Romans 13–16

DAY 2 • *Read* 1 Corinthians 1–4

Say or write your prayer:

1 What do you learn about God and His character in these verses?
2 Where is Jesus in these chapters? Where do you see the gospel?
3 How might you apply these verses to your life?

DAY 3 • *Read* 1 Corinthians 5–9

DAY 4 • *Read* 1 Corinthians 10–12

Say or write your prayer:

1 What do you learn about God and His character in these verses?
2 Where is Jesus in these chapters? Where do you see the gospel?
3 How might you apply these verses to your life?

DAY 5   •   *Read* 1 Corinthians 13–16

DAY 6   •   *Read* 2 Corinthians 1–7

Say or write your prayer:

The Body and All Its Parts

Paul reminds the Corinthians that the body is one unit made up of many parts (1 Cor. 12:12). Though the parts of the body of Christ are made up of varying ethnicities, cultures, genders, and ages, we are unified by the Spirit (1 Cor. 2:13). Unity is the goal, but as we see at the beginning of 1 Corinthians, the church is divided, and some members may value various gifts over others (1 Cor. 1:10–31). Paul uses the imagery of a physical body to provide truth and correction.

The temptation to value certain gifts (and certain people!) over others didn't end with the first-century church. We too are plagued with the same temptation to value certain gifts over and above others. We can forget that God is the giver of gifts, and they are not meant for our glory but for His, as well as for the good of others and service to His church. Let's guard against elevating others because of certain outward gifts as the Corinthians did, and acknowledge God as the giver of all good things.[1]

	Catch up on any missed reading.
IDEAS FOR YOUR REST DAY	Pause to study a text or chapter using your favorite Bible study method.
	Identify a person or situation in the text, and learn more about their story.

A Quick Note: Flying through the New Testament

As you begin this week, you'll soon see—if you haven't noticed already—that the New Testament moves quickly. We've spent most of the year in the Old Testament because it makes up approximately 75 percent of the entire Bible! Weeks 49 to 52 will feel especially quick as we read entire books in one day. The reason for this pace is simple: the time it takes for us to read three chapters in the Old Testament is equivalent to reading an entire epistle in the New. I love listening to the Bible on walks. Recently, I unintentionally listened to three of Paul's epistles.

Why am I pausing to share all of this with you? In the week you are about to enter, your reading will be in six different books. If you feel that you are moving too quickly through a particular book and you'd like to break it up, you could read a few chapters in the morning and then finish the book at night. Another option is to extend the reading beyond 52 weeks. There are no hard and fast rules; the goal is to read and enjoy the Lord. Adjust as you need.

Happy reading!

2 Corinthians 8
to
1 Thessalonians 5

Consider	1 What do you learn about God and His character in these verses?
	2 Where is Jesus in these chapters? Where do you see the gospel?
	3 How might you apply these verses to your life?

DAY 1 • *Read* 2 Corinthians 8–13

....

....

....

....

....

....

DAY 2 • *Read* Galatians 1–6

....

....

....

....

....

....

Say or write your prayer:

1 What do you learn about God and His character in these verses?
2 Where is Jesus in these chapters? Where do you see the gospel?
3 How might you apply these verses to your life?

DAY 3 • *Read* Ephesians 1–6

DAY 4 • *Read* Philippians 1–4

Say or write your prayer:

1 What do you learn about God and His character in these verses?
2 Where is Jesus in these chapters? Where do you see the gospel?
3 How might you apply these verses to your life?

DAY 5 • *Read* Colossians 1–4

DAY 6 • *Read* 1 Thessalonians 1–5

Say or write your prayer:

Grace That Keeps On Giving

If there is an ocean of grace available to us—and there is—we might find much of it proclaimed by the apostle Paul in the first verses of the book of Ephesians. The Greek translation of these first eleven verses is one long sentence, and for good reason! Paul is exasperated by the goodness of God to sinful people. We did not pursue God—He pursued us. And we would never be able to fathom, let alone earn, the spiritual blessings that the Lord bestows upon us: redemption through the blood of Christ, the forgiveness of sin, adoption as sons, everlasting love, an imperishable inheritance, grace upon grace, and so much more. And God achieves this through His own Son.

At least seven times we see Paul referencing God's pursuit of us. The opening praise sets the stage: "Blessed be the God and Father of our Lord Jesus Christ, *who* has blessed us in Christ with every spiritual blessing" (Eph. 1:3). It is God who has blessed us with every spiritual blessing. All the promises of God are yes and amen in Christ (2 Cor. 1:20). God is not withholding anything from you that is not for your absolute best. He has given you and will continue to give you every spiritual blessing. There is only one person qualified to enable access to these spiritual blessings: Jesus Christ.[1]

IDEAS FOR YOUR REST DAY	Catch up on any missed reading.
	Pause to study a text or chapter using your favorite Bible study method.
	Identify a person or situation in the text, and learn more about their story.

2 Thessalonians 1
to
Hebrews 6

1 What do you learn about God and His character in these verses?
2 Where is Jesus in these chapters? Where do you see the gospel?
3 How might you apply these verses to your life?

DAY 1 • *Read* 2 Thessalonians 1–3

DAY 2 • *Read* 1 Timothy 1–6

Say or write your prayer:

1 What do you learn about God and His character in these verses?
2 Where is Jesus in these chapters? Where do you see the gospel?
3 How might you apply these verses to your life?

DAY 3 • *Read* 2 Timothy 1–4

DAY 4 • *Read* Titus 1–3

Say or write your prayer:

Consider

1 What do you learn about God and His character in these verses?

2 Where is Jesus in these chapters? Where do you see the gospel?

3 How might you apply these verses to your life?

DAY 5 • *Read* Philemon

DAY 6 • *Read* Hebrews 1–6

Say or write your prayer:

Go, Make Disciples

When I think of 1 and 2 Timothy and Titus, I think of discipleship. In 1 and 2 Timothy, Paul is writing to his protégé, Timothy. He is teaching him to lead the church—discipling. And Titus could be Christian Living 101. These books have more themes but are very instructive for how we are to relate to one another and the church.

In Titus 2 we see a clear picture of discipling relationships. He is looking for teachers and models but not perfection. So often we think we have to have it all together to teach others. This couldn't be further from the truth. No one would ever teach anyone, ever.

Martha didn't have it together. She was encouraged to rest. But she loved Jesus and He did not condemn her.

Peter denied Christ three times. Not once. Not twice. But three times. And God used him mightily.

Each of us is called to make disciples, but may be hindered by the fear that we aren't smart enough, good enough, or committed enough. There are likely areas where we can grow. But if He is looking for perfect people, He'd find none. He's looking for willing people. So, as we fight our own temptations, we press into relationship with others and learn to make disciples who make disciples.

IDEAS FOR YOUR REST DAY	Catch up on any missed reading.
	Pause to study a text or chapter using your favorite Bible study method.
	Identify a person or situation in the text, and learn more about their story.

Hebrews 7
to
1 John 5

Consider
1 What do you learn about God and His character in these verses?
2 Where is Jesus in these chapters? Where do you see the gospel?
3 How might you apply these verses to your life?

DAY 1 • *Read* Hebrews 7–10

DAY 2 • *Read* Hebrews 11–13

Say or write your prayer:

1 What do you learn about God and His character in these verses?
2 Where is Jesus in these chapters? Where do you see the gospel?
3 How might you apply these verses to your life?

DAY 3 • *Read* James 1–5

DAY 4 • *Read* 1 Peter 1–5

Say or write your prayer:

Consider

1 What do you learn about God and His character in these verses?
2 Where is Jesus in these chapters? Where do you see the gospel?
3 How might you apply these verses to your life?

DAY 5 • *Read* 2 Peter 1–3

DAY 6 • *Read* 1 John 1–5

Say or write your prayer:

| *Purposeful Pain*

S uffering is hard. Trials can be disorienting. But our pain—as with the pain Jesus suffered—has a purpose. Even through our sorrow we know that there's a great and glorious purpose in trials. Suffering is designed to purify our faith.

Peter comforted the Christians in Asia Minor by reminding them (thus reminding us) of the great purpose of suffering. He wrote:

> In this you rejoice, though now for a little while, if necessary, you have been grieved by various trials, so that the tested genuineness of your faith—more precious than gold that perishes though it is tested by fire—may be found to result in praise and glory and honor at the revelation of Jesus Christ. (1 Peter 1:6–7)

In *The Suffering of Man and the Sovereignty of God*, Charles Spurgeon addresses the genuine faith of Job tested by fire and how his faith only reflects the faith that we all desire to have. He writes: "In what better way can the believer reveal his loyalty to his Lord? He evidently follows his Master, not in fair weather only, but in the foulest and roughest ways."[1]

Whether in prosperity or despair, may our words be those of prayer, supplication, and praise to our Father. We will need His power to praise His name.

	Catch up on any missed reading.
IDEAS FOR YOUR REST DAY	Pause to study a text or chapter using your favorite Bible study method.
	Identify a person or situation in the text, and learn more about their story.

2 John

to

Revelation 22

1 What do you learn about God and His character in these verses?

2 Where is Jesus in these chapters? Where do you see the gospel?

3 How might you apply these verses to your life?

DAY 1 • *Read* 2 John, 3 John, Jude

DAY 2 • *Read* Revelation 1–5

Say or write your prayer:

Consider

1 What do you learn about God and His character in these verses?
2 Where is Jesus in these chapters? Where do you see the gospel?
3 How might you apply these verses to your life?

DAY 3 • *Read* Revelation 6–11

DAY 4 • *Read* Revelation 12–16

Say or write your prayer:

1 What do you learn about God and His character in these verses?
2 Where is Jesus in these chapters? Where do you see the gospel?
3 How might you apply these verses to your life?

DAY 5 • *Read* Revelation 17–19

DAY 6 • *Read* Revelation 20–22

Say or write your prayer:

A New Heaven, a New Earth

The book of Revelation is weird and confusing and glorious. I've read it several times and always walk away wondering when the Lord will return and grateful for the life to come with Him forever.

In His kindness, God has given us a picture of what's to come to help us continue in the faith and run this race with endurance. Although you've read it and have likely moved on, I'd like to end our reading plan with this vision in Revelation 21:1–4:

> Then I saw a new heaven and a new earth, for the first heaven and the first earth had passed away, and the sea was no more. And I saw the holy city, new Jerusalem, coming down out of heaven from God, prepared as a bride adorned for her husband. And I heard a loud voice from the throne saying, "Behold, the dwelling place of God is with man. He will dwell with them, and they will be his people, and God himself will be with them as their God. He will wipe away every tear from their eyes, and death shall be no more, neither shall there be mourning, nor crying, nor pain anymore, for the former things have passed away.

May your last Bible reading Rest Day be filled with the knowledge of God and peace that surpasses all understanding.

May you rest knowing that one day He will wipe away every tear by His everlasting love.

IDEAS
FOR YOUR
REST DAY

Catch up on any missed reading.

Pause to study a text or chapter using your favorite Bible study method.

Identify a person or situation in the text, and learn more about their story.

Afterword

We did it! We read the Bible in a year, in two years, or maybe you are still keeping at it but skipped to this page. Wherever you are in the process, I pray that you are more in awe of the Lord today than you were yesterday. I pray that you anticipate growing not only in your understanding of God's Word but also growing in your faith. Any time spent in God's Word is never wasted. Now that you are finished, take a moment to check out the resources for further study, write out a prayer of thanksgiving to the Lord, or start all over again!

In the space below, write out Psalm 103:1–5. Once you've finished writing it out, write out your testimony as a reminder of His work of redemption in your life.

"Bless the LORD, O my soul, and all that is within me, bless his holy name!" (Ps. 103:1)

Additional Resources

Want to keep studying? Here are a few resources that I've used or written that I hope will benefit you.

Commentaries to help with interpretation

The Moody Bible Commentary

The ESV Study Bible

NIV Zondervan Study Bible

Africa Bible Commentary

For Bible study

Women of the Word, Jen Wilkin

Literarily, Kristie Anyabwile

If God Is For Us, Trillia Newbell

A Great Cloud of Witnesses, Trillia Newbell

The Bible Reading Plan

	DAY 1	DAY 2	DAY 3	DAY 4	DAY 5	DAY 6	DAY 7
WEEK 1	Gen. 1–4	Gen. 5–10	Gen. 11–16	Gen. 17–20	Gen. 21–24	Gen. 25–28	Rest & Reflect
WEEK 2	Gen. 29–31	Gen. 32–36	Gen. 37–40	Gen. 41–43	Gen. 44–47	Gen. 48–50	Rest & Reflect
WEEK 3	Ex. 1–4	Ex. 5–8	Ex. 9–11	Ex. 12–14	Ex. 15–17	Ex. 18–21	Rest & Reflect
WEEK 4	Ex. 22–24	Ex. 25–27	Ex. 28–30	Ex. 31–34	Ex. 35–37	Ex. 38–40	Rest & Reflect
WEEK 5	Lev. 1–5	Lev. 6–9	Lev. 10–13	Lev. 14–16	Lev. 17–20	Lev. 21–24	Rest & Reflect
WEEK 6	Lev. 25–27	Num. 1–3	Num. 4–6	Num. 7–8	Num. 9–11	Num. 12–14	Rest & Reflect
WEEK 7	Num. 15–17	Num. 18–20	Num. 21–23	Num. 24–26	Num. 27–30	Num. 31–33	Rest & Reflect
WEEK 8	Num. 34–36	Deut. 1–3	Deut. 4–6	Deut. 7–10	Deut. 11–14	Deut. 15–19	Rest & Reflect
WEEK 9	Deut. 20–24	Deut. 25–28	Deut. 29–31	Deut. 32–34	Josh. 1–4	Josh. 5–8	Rest & Reflect
WEEK 10	Josh. 9–12	Josh. 13–17	Josh. 18–21	Josh. 22–24	Judg. 1–3	Judg. 4–6	Rest & Reflect
WEEK 11	Judg. 7–9	Judg. 10–13	Judg. 14–16	Judg. 17–19	Judg. 20–21	Ruth 1–4	Rest & Reflect
WEEK 12	1 Sam. 1–3	1 Sam. 4–8	1 Sam. 9–11	1 Sam. 12–14	1 Sam. 15–17	1 Sam. 18–20	Rest & Reflect
WEEK 13	1 Sam. 21–23	1 Sam. 24–26	1 Sam. 27–31	2 Sam. 1–3	2 Sam. 4–7	2 Sam. 8–11	Rest & Reflect
WEEK 14	2 Sam. 12–14	2 Sam. 15–17	2 Sam. 18–19	2 Sam. 20–22	2 Sam. 23–24	1 Kings 1–2	Rest & Reflect
WEEK 15	1 Kings 3–6	1 Kings 7–8	1 Kings 9–11	1 Kings 12–14	1 Kings 15–17	1 Kings 18–20	Rest & Reflect
WEEK 16	1 Kings 21–22	2 Kings 1–3	2 Kings 4–6	2 Kings 7–9	2 Kings 10–12	2 Kings 13–15	Rest & Reflect
WEEK 17	2 Kings 16–18	2 Kings 19–21	2 Kings 22–23	2 Kings 24–25	1 Chron. 1–5	1 Chron. 6–9	Rest & Reflect
WEEK 18	1 Chron. 10–14	1 Chron. 15–17	1 Chron. 18–22	1 Chron. 23–26	1 Chron. 27–29	2 Chron. 1–5	Rest & Reflect
WEEK 19	2 Chron. 6–9	2 Chron. 10–15	2 Chron. 16–20	2 Chron. 21–25	2 Chron. 26–29	2 Chron. 30–33	Rest & Reflect
WEEK 20	2 Chron. 34–36	Ezra 1–4	Ezra 5–7	Ezra 8–10	Neh. 1–5	Neh. 6–9	Rest & Reflect

	DAY 1	DAY 2	DAY 3	DAY 4	DAY 5	DAY 6	DAY 7
WEEK 21	Neh. 10–13	Est. 1–5	Est. 6–10	Job 1–5	Job 6–10	Job 11–15	Rest & Reflect
WEEK 22	Job 16–21	Job 22–28	Job 29–32	Job 33–37	Job 38–42	Ps. 1–8	Rest & Reflect
WEEK 23	Ps. 9–15	Ps. 16–19	Ps. 20–26	Ps. 27–32	Ps. 33–36	Ps. 37–40	Rest & Reflect
WEEK 24	Ps. 41–46	Ps. 47–53	Ps. 54–60	Ps. 61–68	Ps. 69–72	Ps. 73–77	Rest & Reflect
WEEK 25	Ps. 78–82	Ps. 83–89	Ps. 90–99	Ps. 100–105	Ps. 106–109	Ps. 110–118	Rest & Reflect
WEEK 26	Ps. 119	Ps. 120–135	Ps. 136–143	Ps. 144–150	Prov. 1–4	Prov. 5–8	Rest & Reflect
WEEK 27	Prov. 9–12	Prov. 13–16	Prov. 17–20	Prov. 21–23	Prov. 24–27	Prov. 28–31	Rest & Reflect
WEEK 28	Eccl. 1–6	Eccl. 7–12	Song 1–4	Song 5–8	Isa. 1–3	Isa. 4–7	Rest & Reflect
WEEK 29	Isa. 8–10	Isa. 11–14	Isa. 15–19	Isa. 20–24	Isa. 25–28	Isa. 29–31	Rest & Reflect
WEEK 30	Isa. 32–35	Isa. 36–38	Isa. 39–41	Isa. 42–44	Isa. 45–47	Isa. 48–50	Rest & Reflect
WEEK 31	Isa. 51–53	Isa. 54–57	Isa. 58–60	Isa. 61–64	Isa. 65–66	Jer. 1–3	Rest & Reflect
WEEK 32	Jer. 4–5	Jer. 6–8	Jer. 9–11	Jer. 12–14	Jer. 15–17	Jer. 18–21	Rest & Reflect
WEEK 33	Jer. 22–24	Jer. 25–27	Jer. 28–30	Jer. 31–32	Jer. 33–35	Jer. 36–38	Rest & Reflect
WEEK 34	Jer. 39–42	Jer. 43–46	Jer. 47–48	Jer. 49–50	Jer. 51–52	Lam. 1–2	Rest & Reflect
WEEK 35	Lam. 3–5	Ezek. 1–4	Ezek. 5–9	Ezek. 10–13	Ezek. 14–16	Ezek. 17–19	Rest & Reflect
WEEK 36	Ezek. 20–21	Ezek. 22–24	Ezek. 25–27	Ezek. 28–30	Ezek. 31–33	Ezek. 34–36	Rest & Reflect
WEEK 37	Ezek. 37–39	Ezek. 40–42	Ezek. 43–45	Ezek. 46–48	Dan. 1–3	Dan. 4–6	Rest & Reflect
WEEK 38	Dan. 7–9	Dan. 10–12	Hos. 1–4	Hos. 5–9	Hos. 10–14	Joel 1–3	Rest & Reflect
WEEK 39	Amos 1–4	Amos 5–9	Obad.	Jonah1–4	Mic. 1–4	Mic. 5–7	Rest & Reflect
WEEK 40	Nahum 1–3	Hab.1–3	Zeph. 1–3	Hag. 1–2	Zech. 1–6	Zech. 7–10	Rest & Reflect
WEEK 41	Zech. 11–14	Mal. 1–4	Matt. 1–5	Matt. 6–9	Matt. 10–12	Matt. 13–15	Rest & Reflect
WEEK 42	Matt. 16–20	Matt. 21–23	Matt. 24–25	Matt. 26–28	Mark 1–4	Mark 5–7	Rest & Reflect
WEEK 43	Mark 8–10	Mark 11–13	Mark 14–16	Luke 1–2	Luke 3–5	Luke 6–7	Rest & Reflect
WEEK 44	Luke 8–9	Luke 10–12	Luke 13–16	Luke 17–19	Luke 20–22	Luke 23–24	Rest & Reflect
WEEK 45	John 1–3	John 4–6	John 7–9	John 10–12	John 13–16	John 17–19	Rest & Reflect

	DAY 1	DAY 2	DAY 3	DAY 4	DAY 5	DAY 6	DAY 7
WEEK 46	John 20–21	Acts 1–4	Acts 5–7	Acts 8–10	Acts 11–14	Acts 15–18	Rest & Reflect
WEEK 47	Acts 19–21	Acts 22–25	Acts 26–28	Rom. 1–4	Rom. 5–8	Rom. 9–12	Rest & Reflect
WEEK 48	Rom. 13–16	1 Cor. 1–4	1 Cor. 5–9	1 Cor. 10–12	1 Cor. 13–16	2 Cor. 1–7	Rest & Reflect
WEEK 49	2 Cor. 8–13	Gal. 1–6	Eph. 1–6	Phil. 1–4	Col. 1–4	1 Thess. 1–5	Rest & Reflect
WEEK 50	2 Thess. 1–3	1 Tim. 1–6	2 Tim. 1–4	Titus 1–3	Philem.	Heb. 1–6	Rest & Reflect
WEEK 51	Heb. 7–10	Heb. 11–13	James 1–5	1 Peter 1–5	2 Peter 1–3	1 John 1–5	Rest & Reflect
WEEK 52	2 John & 3 John, Jude	Rev. 1–5	Rev. 6–11	Rev. 12–16	Rev. 17–19	Rev. 20–22	Rest & Reflect

Biblical Book Abbreviations

LAW

Gen.

Ex.

Lev.

Num.

Deut.

HISTORY

Josh.

Judg.

Ruth

1 and 2 Sam.

1 and 2 Kings

1 and 2 Chron.

Ezra

Neh.

Est.

WISDOM

Job

Ps.

Prov.

Eccl.

Songs

MAJOR PROPHETS

Isa.

Jer.

Lam.

Ezek.

Dan.

MINOR PROPHETS

Hos.

Joel

Amos

Obad.

Jonah

Mic.

Nah.

Hab.

Zeph.

Hag.

Zech.

Mal.

GOSPELS

Matt.

Mark

Luke

John

CHURCH HISTORY

Acts

PAULINE EPISTLES

Rom.

1 Cor.

2 Cor.

Gal.

Eph.

Phil.

Col.

1 Thess.

2 Thess.

1 Tim.

2 Tim.

Titus

Philem.

GENERAL EPISTLES

Heb.

James

1 Peter

2 Peter

1 John

2 John

3 John

Jude

PROPHECY

Rev.

Notes

INTRODUCTION

1. Bob Smietana, "Lifeway Research: Americans Are Fond of the Bible, Don't Actually Read It," Lifeway Research, April 25, 2017, https://research.lifeway.com/2017/04/25/lifeway-research-americans-are-fond-of-the-bible-dont-actually-read-it/.
2. These opening paragraphs have been adapted from *Enjoy: Finding the Freedom to Delight Daily in God's Good Gifts* by Trillia Newbell (Colorado Springs, CO: Multnomah, 2016), 191–92.
3. Of the reading charts and estimates I've found, Chance Faulkner's seemed to be the most realistic for the average reader. Using the ESV's word count for each book of the Bible, he estimated how long it would take to read at a reader's speed of one hundred words per minute. Some people will read slower, some faster, but his estimate seemed to match up with audio Bibles. For example, I saw one chart that suggested that it would only take 1.5 hours to read the book of Genesis, but the audio version for the ESV was 4.56 hours (source: "Genesis," Bible Study Tools, https://www.biblestudytools.com/audio-bible/esv/genesis/), while Faulkner's estimate is approximately 5.30 hours. If you find the idea of reading larger chunks of the Bible overwhelming, I pray that this chart we created based on his data encourages you.
4. Chart content from Chance Faulkner, "How Long Does It Really Take to Read the Bible?," The Gospel Coalition, Canadian Edition, November 18, 2018, https://ca.thegospelcoalition.org/article/how-long-does-it-really-take-to-read-the-bible/. Used by permission.

WEEK 3

1. William Cowper and John Newton, *Olney Hymns in Three Books* (United Kingdom: W. Oliver, 1779), 328.
2. Michael Rydelnik and Michael Vanlaningham, *Moody Bible Commentary* (Chicago: Moody, 2014) 127.

WEEK 6

1. Jay A. Sklar, "Introduction to the Book of Numbers," *NIV Zondervan Study Bible*, ed. D. A. Carson (Grand Rapids, MI: Zondervan, 2015), 239.
2. Kristie Anyabwile, *Literarily: How Understanding Bible Genres Transforms Bible Study* (Chicago: Moody, 2022), 33.

WEEK 8

1. Francis Brown, S. R. Driver, and Charles A. Briggs, *Brown-Driver-Briggs Hebrew and English Lexicon* (Lancaster, TX: Snowball Publishing, 2011), 1033.
2. You can learn more about the Shema through websites dedicated to the Torah. I encourage you to read "The Shema and the Commandment to Love God in Its Ancient Contexts" by Jon D. Levenson, https://www.thetorah.com/article/the-shema-and-the-commandment-to-love-god-in-its-ancient-contexts.

WEEK 9

1. J. I. Packer, *Knowing God* (Downers Grove, IL: InterVarsity Press, 1973), 26.
2. Ibid., 21.
3. Trillia Newbell, *A Great Cloud of Witnesses* (Chicago: Moody, 2021), 86.

A QUICK LOOK AT THE STORYLINE OF THE OLD TESTAMENT

1. This simple outline has been adapted from https://www.watermark.org/blog/bible-timeline. There are many resources available to help you understand the storyline of Scripture. Check out the back of this book for a list of resources.
2. There is some debate whether God was truly silent, which is why I've added quotation marks here.

WEEK 15

1. Tokunboh Adeyemo, *African Bible Commentary: A One-Volume Commentary Written by 70 African Scholars* (Grand Rapids, MI: Zondervan, 2006), 419.

WEEK 20

1. J. Brian Tucker, "Ezra Introduction," *Moody Bible Commentary*, eds. Michael Rydelnik and Michael Vanlaningham (Chicago: Moody, 2014), 638.

WEEK 21

1. William Cowper and John Newton, *Olney Hymns in Three Books* (United Kingdom: W. Oliver, 1779), 328.

WEEK 30

1. Michael Rydelnik and James Spencer, "Isaiah," *The Moody Bible Commentary*, eds. Michael Rydelnik, Michael Vanlaningham (Chicago: Moody, 2014), 1066.

WEEK 35

1. Edward Mote, "On Christ the Solid Rock I Stand," also known as "My Hope Is Built on Nothing Less," 1834, https://hymnary.org/text/my_hope_is_built_on_nothing_less.

WEEK 36

1. Chris Bruno, *The Whole Story of the Bible in 16 Verses* (Wheaton, IL: Crossway, 2015), 83.

WEEK 37

1. R. C. Sproul, *Knowing Scripture* (Downers Grove, IL: InterVarsity Press, 1977), 30.

WEEK 39

1. *The Moody Bible Commentary's* section titled "Purpose" for the book of Obadiah sums up the situation: "The purposes of the book are threefold. Primarily, it is designed to comfort Judah, showing that God will defend them and defeat their enemies. To Edom, and other nations, it is a warning that God will punish them for aggression against Israel. For all believers, it provides consolation in learning that God will defend His people." Steven H. Sanchez, "Obadiah," *The Moody Bible Commentary*, ed. Michael Rydelnik and Michael Vanlaningham (Chicago: Moody, 2014), 1357.

WEEK 47

1. Theologian and ministry leader, Trevin Wax, has a helpful critique about the Romans Road, suggesting that it doesn't begin where it ought to. He suggests, and I agree, that we begin at Romans 1. But for the sake of our Bible reading, the Romans Road continues to be a refreshing read through the gospel. Trevin Wax, "Assuming Too Much in Personal Evangelism," The Gospel Coalition, May 18, 2010, https://www.thegospelcoalition.org/blogs/trevin-wax/assuming-too-much-in-personal-evangelism.

WEEK 48

1. This reflection is adapted from an excerpt of the article by Trillia Newbell, "We Can't Be All Heads," Ligonier, August 13, 2016, https://www.ligonier.org/learn/devotionals/we-cant-be-all-heads.

WEEK 49

1. This reflection is adapted from an excerpt of the article by Trillia Newbell, "The Breathtaking Love We Tend to Forget," Desiring God, February 7, 2019, https://www.desiringgod.org/articles/the-breathtaking-love-we-tend-to-forget.

WEEK 51

1. Charles Spurgeon, *The Suffering of Man and the Sovereignty of God* (Chicago: Fox River Press, 2001), 120.

Refreshingly Deep Bible Studies to Dwell & Delight in God's Word by Trillia Newbell

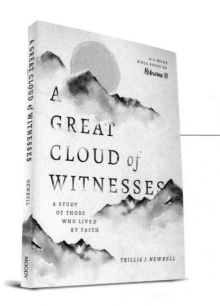

Enter the stories of the faithful in *A Great Cloud of Witnesses*. This six- or eight-week Bible study dives into Hebrews 11, examining the lives of Rahab, Enoch, Gideon, Sarah, and many more whose faiths withstood the tests of their days. By studying the great cloud of witnesses, your own faith will be strengthened to run the race before you.

978-0-8024-2107-4

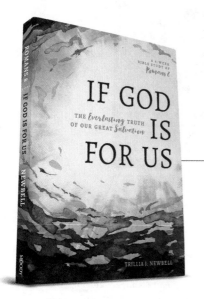

In this 6-week study, Trillia Newbell will walk you through Romans 8 and help you internalize the scandalous truths of our great salvation, our inheritance, the assurance of our faith, and ultimately the love of our good Father.

978-0-8024-1713-8

also available as eBooks

Finding the Peace Your Heart Craves

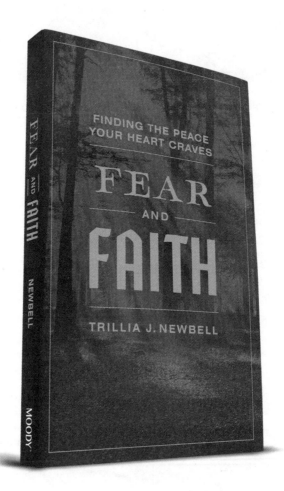